# SKREETLIFE

## The Story of Albert "Cisro" Hampton

Albert Hampton

ISBN: 978-1-966954-96-5 (paperback)
ISBN: 978-1-966954-97-2 (hardcover)
ISBN: 978-1-966954-98-9 (ebook)
Library of Congress Control Number: 2025925330

Printed in the United States of America

# CONTENTS

# CONTENTS

# Chapter 1

All the kids in my neighborhood took The Path to get to school. It was a makeshift dirt pathway that cut through a small forest. Trees lined both sides of The Path, giving us kids some cover from the hot Florida sun. It was an early September morning in 1959, the first time I was ready to take The Path.

I would be a first grader at Dillard Elementary School in Fort Lauderdale, Florida, and I couldn't be more excited. I had a new shirt, pants, and clean shoes. I was nervous but confident on my first day. Even back then, I had a way of making people fall in love with me, and my new teacher would be no different. So, that morning, I got dressed, kissed my mama, and headed towards The Path to start my first day of school.

As I walked, I was joined by my friend Robert. It would be his first day, and I could tell he was nervous. He looked at me and said, "You ready?" in a voice that trembled at the end.

I looked at him with a sly smirk. "I was born ready," I said with a laugh. "What's the worst thing that can happen? You think the teacher gon' eat us or somethin?"

"You don't know!" he shot back.

I looked at him and nudged his shoulder as we walked. "It's gonna be alright, Robert. We got it." He let a half smile creep across his face, and we continued toward the path.

Like I said before, all the kids used The Path to get to school from my neighborhood. Bonnie Lockheart was one of those kids. Bonnie lived on 14th St, and I lived one street over on 14th Ct. He was one of 12 siblings and one of the many boys in his family. His mother and father were hardworking people who provided the best they could for their children. It was more common back then to see two black people married, living together, and raising their family. Like many other faces that took The Path to school, Bonnie was short, with dark brown hair and a clean appearance. He looked just like his father, Bonnie Sr., and people quickly reminded him of that.

Now, this part of the story differs depending on who you ask. Robert and I entered The Path along with Bonnie and his friends. The path's entrance wasn't that wide, maybe enough for one person to enter at a time. As I recall, I arrived first; if you ask Bonnie, he might tell you something different. All I know is that I looked down and saw a black scuff mark across the top of my shoe, and it was on.

I started arguing with Bonnie, and he started arguing with me. Robert joined my side, and his friends joined to help him. Before I knew it, we were throwing fists and kicking feet. After the fight had been going on for a while, Robert and I ran ahead of Bonnie and his friends and started throwing rocks at them.

Robert was one of the best rock throwers I had ever met. He could hit a squirrel going up the side of a tree. I even saw him hit the little flag on the mailbox about 50 feet away. So, we found whatever rocks were alongside The Path and launched them in the boy's direction. I hit most of my targets, but Robert hit all of them. The other kids, who had nothing to do with our dispute, ran along to avoid being caught in the crossfire. Little girls in their new dresses squealed and scolded us for fighting on the first day of school.

Bop! "Ow!" one of the boys cried out as one of the rocks Robert threw hit him square on the side of his cheek.

"Ha!" I yelled as I looked for another rock to throw. Robert was hitting anything that moved, but I was focused on hitting Bonnie.

He was a quick little joker, and it seemed like all my rocks missed him by a hair, but I was determined to get him.

"Missed me, Albert!" he said as another rock I threw zipped by his head and struck a tree. His taunting me only made it worse. I wanted to knock his head off his shoulders with whatever rock I could find.

Even though there were more of them, his friends weren't that good at throwing rocks. Or at least that's what it felt like. They were too busy dodging all of the hits Robert was giving them. It looked like they were even leaning in to make a greater impact when one connected.

"I'm tired of this!" one of Bonnie's friends said after getting hit by one too many rocks.

I wasn't tired, though. I had to get my lick back on Bonnie. And for one moment, when he turned to look at his friend, Bonnie stood still. It was like God had finally allowed me to get my lick.

The rock in my hand was just the right size, smooth, and good enough shape to be carried on the breeze that morning. I didn't hesitate and took my shot. It was almost as if it were in slow motion as I drew back and released the rock in his direction. The rock caught him right on the side of his head.

Bonnie let out a yelp and dropped to his knees. For a second, I was scared. I thought that I hurt him. Maybe I had because when he finally withdrew his hands from the side of his head, I could see a knot forming where the rock hit him.

"Ooooo!" all the nearby children said in unison. I thought the knot was about the size of his head when it probably wasn't any more significant than a dime.

"You're gonna get in trouble," I heard a girl say. "Yo daddy gon kill you," someone else joined in.

Safe to say, the fight was over, and Robert and I won. We straightened our clothes the best we could and headed toward Dillard Elementary. Even though we had the victory, the knot on Bonnie's head wasn't the only one.

I had knots in my stomach all day, thinking about what would happen to me if my father were to find out that I had been fighting on the first day of school. He would wear me out; that was the last thing I wanted.

My father, Lope Hampton, was a disciplinarian in every sense of the word. He was always righteous in dealing with punishment and never whooped us for things we didn't deserve. The thing is, I knew that. I would weigh in my head whether the wrong thing I knew I was about to do was worth the beating my Daddy was gonna put on my behind. Sad to say, the bad thing won out most of the time, but I never blamed him for the beatings because I knew I deserved them. Even though I would run to my mother, Elizabeth, to try to save me from time to time, it hardly ever worked. Daddy did the disciplining, and Mama did the praying. Later in life, I know my mother's prayers kept me out of the grave.

My parents were good people, like most people we lived around. We had just moved to Fort Lauderdale the year before I started first grade, after my father's mother died. We lived in a middle-class black neighborhood where people kept their lawns clean, their children behaved, and they were in church every Sunday. Daddy was a heavy equipment operator, and with his pay, he could care for Mama, me, and the two sisters I had at the time: Rosa, whom we called Chelle, and Audrey, whom we called Penny. He worked hard all day and came home to us. His work ethic is one of the things I admire most about my father. Mama, on the other hand, lived at the church. No matter what was going on, that was where she would be: Sunday School, morning service, cooking meals for after-service, night service, and Bible study. Like many of my friends growing up, Church was like a second home.

Even though we were what people would call middle class, there wasn't a lot of money around. I don't ever remember being hungry, but I don't remember us having more than what we needed. We had enough not to struggle, and we got by on that.

So, as I made my way to Dillard Elementary School that morning, my heart and mind raced. The nerves of the first day of school outweighed my nerves about my father finding out what I had done that morning. The words "Your daddy gon kill you" rang in my head over and over again. I knew the knot on Bonnie's head would be nothing compared to the one on my behind when I got home.

I was tired, dirty, and sweaty when I arrived at my class. I could have cared less about anything the teacher might say because punishment was the only thing on my mind. I sat down at my desk with my head low. I fiddled with my fingers until my teacher came in.

"Good morning, class!" she said as she entered. You could have told me that it was an angel who said those words, and I would have believed you because when I looked up from my desk, I saw the most beautiful woman I had ever seen. Ms. Frankie Forman was a bright-skinned, slim woman. She was dressed as if she were right out of a magazine. She had her hair pinned up and rouge on her cheeks.

I was so stunned that I couldn't answer back, and the rest of the class greeted her with "Good morning." I forgot about the beating I was sure to get when I got back home. I decided to make Ms. Frankie Forman love me if it was the last thing I did. I don't even remember if I got a whopping when I got home that day from school; I just remember the first time I laid eyes on her. She made going to school worth it in my first year. Even though I gave that woman pure hell in that class, I knew she loved me to death. My go-to was fighting, throwing things in class, and making paper airplanes. Ms. Forman would just look at me and shake her head. Sometimes, she would come to my seat and grab me by the ear to make me sit in the corner.

Throughout my early school years, I presented those problems to all my teachers. If they hadn't known me on the first day of school, my name would be all they could say by the end of that first week. I knew I deserved to get in trouble, so they all liked me. I knew what I was doing was wrong and didn't fight the consequences that came with it. It was a mindset that I would maintain for the rest of my life.

But of all the things that I did growing up, the one thing I was known for was fighting. If you stepped foot on 14th Ct, that was my territory, and if you didn't come over there right, your ass was mine. I was always short and skinny, but I'd beat the brakes off anyone, no matter their size. And if they were too big, I'd pick up something and hit them with that. I got a reputation for fighting, and I didn't care. If you messed with me or one of my sisters, you knew I was coming for you. It was only a matter of time before you would have to see me about one of mine.

Once, when I was ten, I was fighting with a boy, and his head hit the side of a car. His eyes rolled back in his head, and he passed out. I got scared and ran away because I knew that he was dead, and I knew my father was going to make me join him when he found out.

I got in so much trouble from my father that it wasn't funny. At least, I didn't think it was funny. Some of the kids in the neighborhood thought it was hilarious how much I used to get in trouble. They would hide out near the window while my father beat me with the belt. I could hear them sniggling under their breath each time the belt hit me. I tried my best not to scream out, to give them nothing to laugh at. After my spanking, I would go outside and find whoever was laughing at me, and now it was their turn to cry. My father would catch me fighting and give me another whooping, and then I was in the house for good.

I didn't stay mad after fights much. Hell, even Bonnie and I became good friends. I guess I had to become friends with Bonnie because most girls lived on my street, and all the boys lived on his. I didn't like playing Jacks or Hopscotch that much, so if I wanted to play with the boys, I would have to make it to 14th Street. Like most kids, Bonnie got over it. Somehow, we started calling him Lump. I don't know how he got that nickname, but I liked to think it was because of that rock I hit him with.

The only other thing I enjoyed more than bringing someone down with my fists was making money. I like to believe I was born a hustler, and I had a mind for business from a young age.

I started my first business at the age of eight. I saved every penny I could by doing little things around the neighborhood to earn money, until I had enough to buy a lawnmower. My father made up the difference for whatever I didn't have. I went to every house on my street and asked them if I could cut their yard, and before long, I was cutting every yard on 14th Ct. Even Mr. Akin, who had his own landscaping business, had me, an eight-year-old, cutting his yard. It was mainly because his wife, who also adored MH, convinced him to do it.

I used to beg Mr. Akin to let me cut yards with him, but he said I was too small. So, I had to wait till I was older to cut yards with him. That didn't stop me from making as much money as I could. Cutting yards and doing odd jobs around my neighbors' houses kept me out of some trouble, and sports did some of the rest.

Even though I would still fight at school or practices, I loved sports. The coaches couldn't get enough of me, so they were willing to put up with some of my violent outbursts: football, basketball, track-and-field, cross country, golf, and swimming. I stayed on someone's team even if I fought the other players. I think I had it in me even to go pro, but something else was calling my name. That something was the streets.

From a young age, I knew that I loved a fast lifestyle. I would see hustlers, gangsters, and business owners with nice cars, lovely homes, and beautiful women, and I knew that was the life for me. I knew I had to get it, and I knew just where to start: 27th Avenue.

# Chapter 2

27th Ave was where it was at! Anyone who was anyone was on 27th Ave. Barbershops, jook joints, bars, gambling, pimps, prostitutes, hustlers, and drug dealers were all there. It was the street that never slept. Back in the 1960s, there weren't many places in Fort Lauderdale where kids my age could hang out. If we weren't playing a game in the yard or working a job, we wouldn't have anything to do but get in trouble.

When I was younger, we would sometimes ride down 27th Avenue to get to church. Mama would shake her head and grimace at all the people sinning in broad daylight. Daddy would nod at his friends and say little. I would be in the back looking at all the people living their lives, and I wanted to be one of them. My father's barber, Mr. Snow, had his barbershop on 27th Ave, and that would be how I could sneak there to get a look up close. While he was getting his hair cut, I would take my time to explore and get a closer look at the people.

I watched the hustlers and gangsters conduct business, and I imagined myself in their shoes one day. I wanted to run things and make money with many beautiful women by my side. The more I hung around, the more the street life mentality embedded itself in my brain, and there was nothing anyone could do to stop it.

One place I couldn't explore was Hick's Pool Room. That's where the real action was. All the high rollers would go into Hick's to play a game of pool. Even if they didn't play, they could watch a game or bet on other people playing. I was too young to go in, so the best I could do was watch the people through the window. I would spend all day on the corner next to Hick's, watching the people go in and out and trying to figure out a way to get inside. I was always short and skinny, so there was no way to fake my age; therefore, it was the outside that mattered to me. I would be outside until the streetlights came on, and then I would have to go home.

The first time I saw pool played, I was taken with the game. I was struck by how much skill those men needed to make those shots and sink those balls. The game was so intense that I didn't want to breathe, as I didn't want to startle the men or mess up the match. I visited the library and began reading about the game, which greatly piqued my interest. I was gonna be a pro before I got a chance to pick up a cue.

When I was thirteen, I finally got my chance to get inside Hick's. The man who ran the Hall was called Chocolate. I guess he got that nickname because he was big and dark-skinned. He knew me from always hanging around the pool hall, and went to Snow to get his hair cut. He decided to offer me a job keeping the pool hall clean. I almost leaped out of my skin when he asked me. I was so excited. I knew this would be my way in and wouldn't mess it up. I was responsible for keeping track of the games and ensuring that everyone paid when their time was up. It was ten cents a game back then, and once you got to a dollar, it was time to pay up.

Chocolate told me that if he were next door, hanging out at Snow's, and somebody refused to pay, to get him. I had to do it a couple of times. Some folks didn't take too kindly to a scrawny little kid telling them it was time to pay up, but when Chocolate came through the door, they found the money, and they found it quick. I also had the job of doing maintenance around the hall. I would sweep up, ensure the cues were lined up nicely, and rack all the balls, then wait for the next customer to take a table. I loved it. I was exactly where I wanted to be. Everyday after school, I was heading to Hick's instead of home.

During the slow times, Chocolate let me practice on one of the tables in the back of the hall. This is where I applied what I had learned from the books I had been reading. I would practice as long as I could every day until a customer arrived. Chocolate had been watching me practice, and he noticed I had a knack for the game.

"Who taught you how to play?" Chocolate said to me on one slow afternoon. I was working on a trick shot I saw in a book and couldn't quite get it right.

"Nobody," I said. "I read some books and have been watching others play for a while."

"Well," he said. "It looks like you have some potential. You could be really good at this game."

"Yes, sir," I said as I took the shot. I missed it. "Damn," I mumbled under my breath.

"You know why you missed that shot?" Chocolate said. "You were nervous. That's something you can't be when you play this game. If you get nervous, you've already lost."

The next time I went for the shot, I took a deep breath and calmed down. I sunk it.

"See," Chocolate said, "You just gotta be confident at all times."

I took that advice to heart. I would be confident with any shot, too. That's how it worked for a while. I would work at the pool hall, and when I had downtime, Chocolate would give me pointers on how to improve my game. He told me about a famous Black pool player named Cicero Murphy. He was the first Black person to win both U.S. titles and world titles. He was a bad boy. He could run two hundred balls, miss a shot, and then run another two hundred. This was a massive deal because, just like today, back then, the pool was dominated by other races, and black people were not considered champions. To see this man become one of the best in the world was truly remarkable. I made it my mission to become the Cicero of the South.

Chocolate started calling me Cicero because I was getting so good. Eventually, everyone started calling me that nickname, which still sticks with me. To this day, most people know me by my nickname, Cicero, rather than my given name, Albert.

By the time I played my first real game, I wasn't nervous at all. I beat the boy so bad that I don't remember his name or even what he looked like. He might have been one of the balls I sunk into the holes.

Word started getting around about the boy at Hick's that was beating everyone in the pool. That drew interest and made people want to play against me. I remember the first time I played for money. It was one of the local hustlers, and he had something to prove. He didn't think this little scrawny kid who sweeps up around the tables could play anywhere in his vicinity.

"What you got to put up, little nigga?" he said. "You got some lunch money?" The people around the pool hall laughed, but I didn't let it shake me. I kept what Chocolate told me in my head, and I kept calm. I pulled out the little five dollars I had in my pocket and put it on the table without a word.

Everyone laughed. People were used to playing for car note payments and diamond rings, and here I was with literal lunch money. I didn't get shaken; I kept telling myself to stay calm and play the game.

The hustler didn't take me seriously at first. He laughed and joked around with people and didn't make a big deal out of it when he missed a couple of shots, but I took it seriously. The pockets on the pool table may as well have been as big as craters on the moon. I was sinking every shot. When I won our first game, he chalked it up to him not paying attention, but I was happy to have ten dollars now.

"You wanna double that change?" he said to me. "I can't let you think you got one up on me."

"Yup," I said. I stayed cool and calm. It was gonna be just like the first game for me.

The hustler was paying attention this time. He didn't flirt with any women who walked by; he didn't stop to relight his cigarette or spend time talking between shots. He watched the table like his life depended on it.

He did try to intimidate me. He would try to yell out things and tell me to take my time when a tricky shot was coming, but I didn't get rattled. I whooped him worse when he was paying attention than when he was just having fun. His pride was hurt, but he told me I was excellent.

Soon, other people wanted to try to beat me, and I started making a good chunk of money off of beating people in pool. That success did come with some drawbacks. People stopped wanting to play against me because I was so good. If they did want to play against me, they wanted me to give them a ball (to let them play with fewer balls on the table) or bet me on how many balls I could win by. That made playing less fun, but I still loved the game.

I even started going to other pool halls around Fort Lauderdale and challenging the best players there. We didn't always play for money, but I still wanted to boast that I was the best pool player in the South.

Even though I was whooping everyone who stepped up to me, there was one person whom I could never beat. Chocolate would whoop me in a game without even batting an eye. No matter how I studied his game, I couldn't keep up with it. "Keep playing," he said. "You'll get there one day. I might not be there to see it, but you'll get there," He would laugh, but I was determined to beat him one day.

Around the time I started playing pool and making money, I lost most of my interest in school. I may have dropped out earlier if it weren't for other sports. Even though Chocolate and the other grown people didn't mind me not attending school, my parents were something else.

When I started going to 27th Ave, I stopped wanting to be home. I felt like nothing at home was of interest to me. Mama and Daddy began to have more children, and by the time I started going to 27th Avenue, Janice, April, and Elizabeth had all arrived. The house was loud, with little girls running everywhere, and I wanted to be a grown man. So, every chance I got, I would be away from home. Either down on the Ave or over to one of my friends' houses.

I recall when my father discovered that I had stopped attending school. He and Mr. Snow were good friends at the time, and he happened to mention to my father that he had seen me going into the pool hall almost every day, even when I was supposed to be at school. I don't blame him for telling on me,  he was honest with his friend.

That day, my father confronted me about my absence from school. "I know why your grades are so bad," he said.

"Yes, sir?" I said. A knot formed in my stomach as I looked at my father. When I was younger, even his stare of disapproval was enough to send shivers down my spine, but when I got older, that stare made me shiver less and less. When my father confronted me, I was probably making more money than he was by playing pool. So, I was ready for whatever he said or tried to do.

"You have been down there to that pool hall every day instead of to that school!" he said.

"Yes, sir," I responded.

"What do you think you are going to do? Huh? You think you gon' get far in this world without education?"

"I don't know," I said as I shrugged. I looked down at the floor to avoid his disapproval.

He grabbed my chin so my eyes could meet his. "In my house, you go to school. You ain't grown, and you don't have a say about what happens around here."

"I'm not going back to school," I said. My heart was pounding, but I was ready for whatever came next.

When my father looked at me, I could tell by the look in his eyes that he already knew that I was gone. There was nothing that he could say, and no beating that he could give me that was gonna make me go back to school.

He sighed and said, "You go to school or find somewhere else to stay." "Yes, sir," I said. My heart was still beating fast as my father walked away.

I was now gonna have to prove how old I was. I packed up all the clothes that I could and left the house. Mama almost made me wanna stay. I could barely stand to see her upset, but I knew that I had to get out and do things on my own. I didn't know how I was going to do it, but I had the know-how to get it done.

From the pool hall, I met a man we called Fido. He was a boxer in the service and owned a store. Above that store, there was a small apartment. Fido and his wife agreed to let me stay in the apartment, and I would use my winnings from playing pool to pay them rent.

Fido became a father figure to me, and his beautiful wife, a surrogate mother. They ensured that I did everything I needed to get by and did what I could to get them their money at the beginning of the month. It worked out well most of the time, but when people know you're good at the game, they don't want to play you anymore.

By the time 1970 rolled around, I had won the Florida South Young Adult Pool Championship three times and was making about $50 a day playing pool. But when you're a young champion, people start hedging their bets when you play them. They want you to give them two or three balls and put all these rules on what you must do to win.

The kids I hung around with thought I was the coolest person on Earth. I had the best clothes, jewelry, and some fame, and I was doing things they could only dream of.

One of my school friends, Bruce, was also a pool player. In the 7th grade, after his mother passed away, he moved from Ocala, a small city in central Florida, to Fort Lauderdale. He was a big, dark boy with the nickname Big Man. Bruce was good, but since he decided to stay in school, he didn't get as good as I did.

I recall that, in the 1969 Florida South Young Adult Pool Championship, I was eliminated in an early round without paying attention. I made stupid mistakes and lost my chance to win for three consecutive years. Bruce made it to the end, though. He was a great pool player, and most of the time, he would be the only person to put me on the ropes and beat me. However, for some reason, he was struggling in the final round.

I couldn't let him lose. We had to take another championship back to Hick's. Plus, the boy he was playing against was someone we used to beat regularly. He couldn't have gotten this far and choked.

"What are you doing?" I said when he missed a shot. "You gonna let this scrub beat you?" Jeff shot me a cold look like he wasn't in the mood, but I didn't care. I couldn't let him lose. "Get your head in the game, man, beat this nigga."

"Let me play the game," Bruce said. I could tell he was aggravated.

I didn't let up, though. I kept egging him on, and it worked. Bruce played like I knew he could play, and we brought home another championship to Hick's.

"Man, you made it," Bruce told me one day. We were playing a friendly game of pool in the back of Hick's.

"Yeah," I responded, focusing on the striped 12 ball. "I guess I did! Getting into my own place was the best thing I could have ever done. I get to set my own rules and do anything I want. Ain't nobody trying to run me down to go home and no school after me about gettin' no grades."

"I hear ya," Bruce said. "I can't wait til I get out on my own."

"What's stoppin' ya? You are good enough at playing pool to make some good money."

"Nah. I think I'm gonna finish out high school." I sighed, "More money for me then."

As I mentioned earlier, the money I earned from playing pool was quite substantial. $50 a day went a long way back in the early 1970s, but I wanted more. 27th Ave had some real big-timers there, and while I may have been a big shot to the kids I went to school with, I was nothing compared to them. They had clothes that looked like they came straight off the runway, rings on every finger, and cars fresh off the showroom floor. I wanted that; hell, I needed that.

I started smoking marijuana at the young age of 12 when I first started hanging out on 27th Ave. So, I realized that another quick way to make money was to start selling some on the side. So, I joined the drug dealers on the corners of 27th Ave, and that started bringing in more money. My personality made me attractive to customers. I could persuade someone to buy more than they intended to buy. If you wanted to buy a nickel bag, I could talk you into purchasing a dime.

So, my clothes started getting nicer, my jewelry became brighter, and I could afford a nice car; life was perfect.

One day, Bruce introduced me to his cousin, Donald Thompson, whom we affectionately called Nut. Nut was a short, dark-skinned boy from New York who came down to Fort Lauderdale to show us country boys how it was done in the big city.

"Ya'll country niggas don't know nothin' about this!" he said as he waved a bag of white powder around.

"Nigga, I done seen cocaine before," I shot back.

"This ain't no cocaine!" he said. "This is Smack, Nigga! Heroin"

I had seen heroin as well, but I never tried it. I had seen too many people strung out. "Nah, man, I ain't tryna be out here like that."

"See," Nut said, "Yall country niggas don't know how to handle y'all shit. You won't be strung out on the streets if you do it right. You gotta know how to do things in moderation."

Bruce and I looked at each other. We were both nervous about trying the drug, but neither one of us wanted to look like scared country bumpkins in front of Nut. So we both agreed to try some smack.

Nut prepared the heroin and loaded up the needle. He tied my arm off and told me to relax. I winced as the needle broke the skin and entered my arm. I watched as the white powder transformed into a brownish liquid that entered my veins. I didn't know what to expect, but nothing could compare to the feelings I experienced. It was as if Nut had shot pure gold into my arm and was now spreading through my entire body. I thought this must be how the angels feel. I couldn't be touched when I was high, and when I came down, all I knew was that I wanted another hit.

Nut was proper about that one thing, Us country niggas didn't know how to handle our shit. Heroin became a way of life for me. Any money that I got was going toward feeding my habit. I couldn't sell enough weed or win enough in the pool to help feed it. Like most other addicts, I was chasing that first high. I wanted to feel like an angel again. I wanted to have gold running through my veins.

My habit got bad when Fido died. My surrogate father was many things. He was a boxer, a business owner, and a card shark, but none of that led to his death. He was just in the wrong place at the wrong time.

Some white boys got into a fight at one of the bars on 27th Ave and got beaten up. When they left, Fido went into the bar to have a drink. Those white boys decided to return to the bar and shoot it up. Fido just happened to be at the bar and was hit by a bullet that wasn't meant for him.

When I was headed home that night, I saw all the ambulances and police cars surrounding the bar.

"What happened, man?" I asked a man in the crowd forming around the police barricade.

"It's Fido," he said, "Them crackas done killed Fido."

My heart sank in my chest, and I could barely breathe. I had just seen him earlier and didn't think something could happen to him. I wanted to find those white boys and send them to the same place they sent Fido.

Fido's death hit me like a ton of bricks, and the only thing that could help ease the pain was heroin. My habit was now costing more money than I could make. So, I had to resort to alternative means to earn money.

Nut, who was also addicted, and I started stealing anything we could get our hands on to feed our habit. Delivery trucks would stop on the side of the road, and the drivers would go into the store for a break, and that was our chance. We stole everything that wasn't attached to the floor. One time, we stole house phones.

" What are we gonna do with these?" I asked Nut. "Shit, people will buy them!" he said.

He was right. We always found somebody to buy whatever we stole, and we always had enough to feed our addiction.

I stayed away from home, ashamed of what I had become and how I lived. I was starting to remind myself of the worst parts of my father. Now, Lope Hampton didn't do hard drugs, but he did like his whiskey. He would get so drunk sometimes that he would make a spectacle out of himself in front of everyone. I have memories of my mother and my sister trying to coax him inside while he was so drunk he could hardly stand. Mama would cry, and Rosa would plead for him to come inside.

I fooled myself into thinking that I was somehow better than my father because I kept it away from my family, but I was just hiding my shame. I was functioning, and no one could tell that I was battling a similar demon to my father and was no different from him at all.

I would cheat people out of their money. I would sell them oregano and tell them it was weed, I would put baby powder in a bag and make people think it was cocaine, and by the time they realized they had been fooled, I was long gone. One time, I even tricked this white boy into thinking I had sold him one hundred dollars' worth of weed when it was an empty bag. I knew if he had caught me, he would have killed me. I didn't care, I just had to feed that addiction that was slowly killing me.

Around this same time, a man named Charlie B. started hanging around Hick's Pool Room. Like Nut, he was also from New York. He had the big rings, fancy cars, and fine women everyone had, but he was also something else. He was a big-time heroin dealer, and as someone who was a hustler, I knew that the money that I could make dealing heroin would put the money I was making dealing marijuana to shame. He would drop vast amounts of money on pool games, and even when he lost, it didn't seem to bother him. He would even laugh at losing money. That's how I knew he had real money, and not what the hustlers around 27th Ave called real money.

I approached Charlie B. one day and asked if I could sell on his behalf. He was hesitant at first. I was still so young, and I was trying to mask a very prevalent cocaine addiction. I guess it must have been something about my charm that got me into his good graces because he surprisingly agreed to let me sell for him.

Well, I didn't waste any time. I immediately started using all of the heroin that Charlie B. gave me. When it was all gone, reality kicked in. Charlie B. was nice enough. He was always friendly and had something nice to say to people, but he was a big-time dope dealer, and I knew he didn't play about his money. I was just this skinny little heroin addict who just messed up a lot of money for him. So, I decided to make myself as scarce as possible.

For the first time since I was thirteen, I stayed away from 27th Ave. If I thought I saw a car that looked anything like the car that Charlie B. drove, I would run down the nearest alley or hop over the nearest fence. I would tell everyone to inform Charlie B. that they haven't seen me and don't know where I was. I tried to become a ghost. Even Chocolate started worrying about me.

He was concerned that I had given up on becoming the next greatest pool player. I couldn't even worry about that; I was too afraid I wouldn't live to be twenty, let alone an adult champion pool player.

After hiding away from Charlie B. for about a month, I decided to confront him. I got myself together and went into Hick's one night when I knew that he was going to be there and face whatever fate was coming for me. I was tired of always looking over my shoulder; anything had to be better than the paranoia.

Charlie B. was sitting in the corner with the other hustlers and looked in a good mood. This is an excellent time to approach him.

"Well, damn!" he said as I walked up. I had my head down to avoid looking him in the eye. "Is this a ghost I see? Is that you, Cicero?"

I kept my eyes on the floor and rocked on my shoes. I must have looked like a real child at that moment. It could save me from whatever he had in mind. "Yeah, it's me," I said. "Can we talk?"

"Yeah," Charlie B. said. He got up from the table and headed toward the exit. His rings sparkled in the light of the pool hall as we made our way outside.

When we got to a place where we could talk without being heard, I tried to cop my plea. "I'm sorry!" I blurted out. "Man, I gotta problem, and I didn't mean to mess up what you gave me. I just needed a fix, and…"

Charlie B. put his hand up to stop me from talking. "You think I didn't know what you did?" My heart was beating out of my chest. "I know a junkie when I see one. When you disappeared from around here, I knew one of two things had to happen: either you ran off with the money, or you ran off with the drugs. And since I been hearin' about how you and ya' little friend been stealing anything that ain't nailed down, I knew it had to be the drugs."

"I'm sorry. I'll get you your money! I just…"

"Don't even worry about it, young blood," Charlie B. put his hand on my shoulder. I know how it can be. That shit, get ahold of you and won't let go." "You too?" I looked him in the eye for the first time. I could see that he understood what I was going through.

"Yeah, me too." He patted my shoulder and then removed his hand. "I just know not to fuck over the people that I get my shit from." My heart started beating fast again. "Just be lucky it was me. Somebody else wouldn't have gone as easy."

From that day forward, Charlie B. became like another father figure. He replaced the relationship I lost with Fido and gave me greater insight into operating in the streets. I looked up to him and learned how to feed my addiction without it controlling me. But all things have to come to an end, and that is especially true when you're working on the streets.

Charlie B. met the same fate that all drug dealers meet. He was arrested for possession and taken to jail. Since Charlie was also an addict, the withdrawals in jail were kicking his ass.

Police didn't care about a drug dealer going through withdrawals, so they didn't make sure he got the medicine he needed when going through heavy withdrawals. Charlie B. ended up dying right there on the floor of his cell.

The news of Charlie dying hit me like a ton of bricks. Another father figure I had clung to was gone, and I began to spiral out of control. I started committing more crimes and robbing more people to get my fix. I got sloppy, and I got more violent. Growing up, I was always ready to fight, which didn't change when I got out alone. I started throwing bullets instead of throwing rocks like I did with Lump. I was known to carry a gun, and I wasn't afraid to pull it out at any time I needed to. My reputation for pulling out a gun was almost as big as my reputation for playing pool, and I didn't care.

One night, Nut and I broke into my old high school to steal typewriters, books, and instruments. Since schools didn't have camera systems back then, we thought we were in the clear. Little did I know that a girl named Diane Lee saw Nut, and I walked away from the crime scene.

I knew Diane from growing up and attending school together. Her brothers and I used to play football together before I stopped attending school. So, when she told the police that she saw me leaving the school carrying the instruments, I knew who I had to get. I wanted to hurt Diane badly. I wanted to pistol-whip or something else to let her know to keep her mouth shut, but as luck would have it, I could never catch up to her.

So, now I was sitting in court and being sentenced to three years in prison, six days before my eighteenth birthday.

# Chapter 3

I had played pool with some big-time hustlers and even got threatened by a couple when they thought I hustled them. I had stolen a lot of things. One day, I almost ran into my mother's car when I snatched a lady's purse. I had survived countless whoopings from Lope Hampton, but I had never been as scared as when I went to Lake Butler Prison on December 20, 1971.

Lake Butler was like something out of a movie. The prisoners and the guards seemed to always walk around on edge. I picked up on the energy the place had as soon as I arrived. I knew you were not to mess around with anyone at any time. The prisoners were one thing. There were gangs and cliques of people who hung around each other for protection. People made wine in their cells and smuggled in contraband. White people stayed with their kind, and the Black people stayed with theirs.

The guards were different. It was almost like they were looking for problems with the inmates. If you looked them in the eye or even in their direction for too long, you were now on their radar, and that is not where you wanted to be. They especially had it out for people from Miami. That was like printing a target on the front of your uniform. The slightest infraction would be grounds for a beating if you were from Miami. Being from Fort Lauderdale, I kept a low profile in case they thought it was close enough.

You didn't speak to a guard unless you were spoken to. They took that as disrespect or a sign that you were trying to get familiar with them. Either way, you could be beaten senseless for that. If an inmate saw you talking to a guard for too long, they would think that you were snitching, and you could be beaten or killed by them. It was a dangerous game that you didn't want to play. Your best bet was to keep to yourself as much as possible and only talk to people when they talked to you, but not for too long. It's how I survived.

I remember a guy in the cell next to mine didn't pick up on the energy of the prison fast enough, and he was quickly taught about how things went.

As I lay in bed one night, I heard keys rattling in front of the cell beside mine.I knew what was coming. The man in the cell had made a joke with one of the guards earlier that day. It was harmless, but he didn't know that having fun at Lake Butler was prohibited. What made it even worse was some of the other inmates laughed. I grabbed my pillow a little tighter as I heard the door to the cell creak open.

"You think you're Richard Pryor or somebody?" I heard a voice say. I knew exactly who it was. While most of the guards at Lake Butler were white men with a chip on their shoulders, there was one Black man. We called him Nigga Charlie. I don't remember his full name, and he doesn't deserve the recognition. While all the guards were terrible, he seemed to go out of his way to be a bit more cruel than the others, especially to the other Black people. It was like he had something to prove to the other guards, like he was one of them and not one of us.

He was tall and broad with a bald head. He looked like he ate a bowl of nails every morning with the look he had on his face. Well, at least that was the look he gave the inmates. He only showed his teeth when talking to the other guards, and it looked like he was different. It was like all the hate had gone away, and he was almost pleasant to be around. But you didn't want to let him catch you looking at him. That would put you in his sights and be on the list for a beating. He always planted his hand on his nightstick like waiting to use it.

"Huh?" I heard the man in the cell next to me say. It was either late at night or early in the morning, and he was half asleep. He was going to find out that joking was a punishable offense.

I heard the first whack of the nightstick come down on the man, and I knew it had to break a bone. The sound of the cracking was only drowned out by the sound of the man's howls of pain. I tried to cover my head with my pillow, but it was like the guards beat him harder so that no one could escape the noise.

It seemed like it lasted for hours. They would take turns whacking the man and yelling any horrible thing they could think of as he screamed and pleaded for his life. I pleaded with God to either let the man die or for him to pass out so his torture could end. After that, the man was taken to the infirmary, and I never saw him again.

That beating put the already on-edge people in the prison even more on edge. They would threaten other inmates and say they would suffer the same fate as the jokester if they got out of line. Rumors spread that the man was now a vegetable and had to be fed through a tube. Some people say he got moved to the mental ward because he suffered brain damage, and others said he died in the infirmary, and the guards blamed his wounds on the other inmates. Either way, no one wanted to find out or join the man, so the prison was quiet.

I didn't think I would make it out of Lake Butler alive, but I was thrown a lifeline. In March of 1973, I heard I would be moved into a youth program. The state of Florida wanted to rehabilitate me so I wouldn't turn into a hardened criminal, and that was definitely going to happen if I stayed in Lake Butler. I was one of twelve youths who would be moved into a program across Florida. I was told the program I would be in was the best because it was in Daytona Beach, FL.

I was part of the first class of juveniles to attend the ACI Youth Aversion Program in Daytona Beach. The facility wasn't right on the beach, but it was close enough. You could smell the sea air coming off the ocean, and it was like the air breathed something new into me. All the stealing, dealing, cheating, and using I did on 27th Ave was carried away on the salty air.

At ACI, we didn't have strict and violent correctional officers. Instead, we had counselors. These people were trained to listen to us and figure out why we did what we did so they could try to steer us away from a life of crime. These people cared and seemed like they weren't just there for a check.

J.D. Thomas was the counselor assigned to me. I came to find out he wanted me specifically. He was a tall white man with blonde hair and blue eyes. He was a former military man who talked sternly but had a soft heart. He and his wife lived at ACI, and they treated all of us, especially me, like family. Since I was the oldest of all the kids there, on my way to nineteen, Mr. Thomas emphasized my being a good role model for the kids. "Hampton!" he would say as he slapped his hand down on my shoulder, "You gotta be good so these boys can be great." I would swell up with pride and make sure I walked a little taller around the other boys.

I made friends there from all over the state of Florida. One of them was a white boy from Cocoa Beach named Tony Morris, who followed me around like I was the boss. I thought I was terrible; he was even worse.

He was stealing and beating people up, but unlike me, he was fascinated with fire, which landed him here. I always wondered whether he went through somewhere like Lake Butler or if they sent him straight here. Mr. Thomas said that I made him act better and took that to heart.

They had a pool table at ACI, and I couldn't pass up the opportunity to show these people why I was the champ. I whooped everybody on campus who dared step up to the table. I got bored beating everyone, so I would give lessons to some of the kids, so there would be some competition.

Even though I couldn't play them for money, I did play them for their food. Especially if there was something good cooking in the kitchen, I would have their dessert at dinner.

ACI was a community program, which meant we were right there in the community. We didn't have bars on our windows or uniforms we had to wear. It was almost like we were at a summer camp. I could return to school and finish what I left in Fort Lauderdale during my time there. Mr. Thomas had me speak to local kids about my experiences to dissuade them from following a similar path. I got a job working in the kitchen at ACI with a woman named Ms. Costella, and like everyone else, she fell in love with me. I would help her prepare all the meals for everyone in the program, and I did prep work for her so her workload was more manageable.

ACI also helped me kick my heroin addiction. Being there around all that support, I could kick it cold turkey. I was no longer the junky willing to steal anything or do anything trying to chase that high. I was a new man. I started talking to my parents more often than when I lived in the same city with them. My mother was happy I was making a change, and my father was proud of me. For the first time, I felt like a good son. Those phone calls and letters made me feel like I was in the house with them and was their little boy again. I found a new respect for my father, and after battling my addiction, I saw how alcohol had hold of him, and I didn't judge him as much. I figured he needed the time to sort himself out like I did.

Everything was going great at ACI until I got a phone call from my parents. It wasn't bad news; it was great news, possibly the best news I had received so far in my life. I was going to be a big brother. I was already a big brother to four little sisters, but this time, it would be a brother. For all my life, my family had been overrun by women. Part of the reason I stayed away from home was that I had little girls running around all the time. Now, there would be more men around than just me and Daddy.

I wanted to be home for the first time in a long time—not just in Fort Lauderdale, not even on 27th Ave, but back in my parents' house on 14th CT with all the little girls running around. I wanted to be there when my mother gave birth, and I wanted to be in the hospital to welcome my little brother into the world.

I made up my mind to leave ACI when my mother gave birth, and I wasn't there. The family was growing and leaving me behind. I wouldn't have it, so I had to go back home. My little brother was two months old, and in the phone calls I would have with my mother, I could hear him in the background, and it only made me yearn to leave even more.

One morning, I set my alarm clock so my roommate could get up on time, and I just walked out of ACI.

I knew it would be a matter of time before my friends and counselors noticed that I'd slipped away. I walked around downtown Daytona for a while and thought about how to get out of town. When I saw a few too many police cars riding down the street, I knew they were out looking for me, so I took the little money I had from Ms. Consuela and caught a bus to Fort Pierce. My heart beat like a drum as I left Daytona and all the good I had done at ACI, but the thought of a little brother drove me home.

I didn't have enough money at my next stop in Fort Pierce to make it home, so I just sat in the train station for a while, trying to figure out what to do. The man working behind the register in the train station looked nice enough, so I asked him if he had any work I could do.

"Excuse me, Sir," I said. I tried to look as pitiful and apologetic as I could. "Yeah," the man said. I could tell he was annoyed. The bus station was busy that day, and he barely had time to talk.

"Sir, I'm trying to get home to see my mother, and I don't have enough money to make it there. Is there anything I could do for you to earn my fare?" The man looked at me, and I could tell he was aggravated. His white shirt was starting to show sweat stains from all the running he had been doing all day, and his glasses were getting fogged from all his heavy breathing. "I tell you what," he said in a huff, "if you can clean the bathrooms for me, I'll give you five dollars."

"Five dollars?!" I wanted to scream out, but it was more money than I had, and I couldn't stay around much longer. The police would be on to me in no time. "Thank you," I said. The man handed me the cleaning supplies, and I cleaned the bathrooms. All my work was worth at least twelve times five dollars, but the man paid me what he owed me.

I sat back down in a corner stall at the bus station, deciding what to do. I knew returning to the man and asking for more money wouldn't work. He was already aggravated. Then, God provided me with a ram in the bush. The man working behind the concession counter had left the register open when he went to the back of the store to get something. I looked around, and everyone seemed too busy looking for things to buy or checking the time of their departures, so I took my chance.

I eased behind the counter and over to the cash register, looking as calm as possible. People saw me cleaning the restrooms, so for all they knew, I worked there. I could still hear the man in the back looking for something, but I knew I had to be quick.

The cash register was full of money—there had to be over five hundred dollars present—but I wasn't a fool. If I took all the money, the man would know something was wrong, and I would be caught. So, I took what I thought was owed for cleaning those nasty bathrooms. So, I removed sixty dollars from the register and returned my seat in the booth.

When the man returned to the register, he was too flustered or didn't notice that the money was gone.

After escaping my crime, I went to the ticket counter and purchased a ticket to Fort Lauderdale.

We had to stop at every place between Fort Pierce and Fort Lauderdale on the map. That was the longest bus ride I had ever taken in my life. When I finally reached home, it was two o'clock in the morning.

When I knocked on the door, I expected my parents to be happy to see me, but they were anything but happy. My father barely spoke to me, and my mother had visible traces of tears in her eyes. The people from ACI had already told her that I escaped and to bring me back before the police found me. I didn't care. I just had to see my baby brother.

My mother brought him out, and I held baby Curtis for the first time. Sitting in my father's chair with my brother in my arms, I could only look at him. He was another Hampton man about to be released into the world. Would he be like me, or would he be like Daddy? Or would he do something different from both of us?

"Baby," my mother said as she sat on the couch before me, "you know you gotta go back, right?"

I held Curtis tighter and looked up at Mama. She was tired and disappointed from worrying about me over the past day or the past few years. "I can't go back, Mama," I said. I kept my head down to avoid her eyes. "If the police catch you down here, you won't have a choice," she said.

"They'll take you to jail, and you'll back in Lake Butler."

The words of that prison sent a chill down my spine. "I'll run," I said. "Run where? Back to 27th Ave? Back to the hustling, the stealing, thegambling, and the drugs?"

My head sank deeper with every word she said. "I can't go back, Mama." "Why not? Why can't you go back? You were doing so well. Your daddy and I were so proud of you. I've been bragging about how well you've been doing and how God will use you to be a testimony for other people. Why would you throw that all away?" "I just can't," was all I could say.

We went back and forth like that over the next couple of hours. Mama tried convincing me, and I was determined to never step back in ACI. I could never give her or myself a good reason not to return. I didn't want to go back to Lake Butler, and I knew it was only a matter of time before the police tracked me down and I would be in prison again.

"Is there anything you've ever asked me for that I didn't do?" My mother said she was exhausted with me. "Anything? Even the clothes off my back, even my life, I would give for anyone else in this family!" Tears streamed down her face as her heart broke.

I couldn't stand seeing my mother cry, so I conceded and returned to ACI. My mother was happy; she didn't even leave her housecoat. She told me to lie in the car's back seat and drove me back to Daytona Beach for four hours.

When I walked in the door of the main ACI building, my stomach was in knots, and my head hung low out of embarrassment and shame for what I had done. My mother told me to face my responsibilities like the man I was, and I was determined to do that.

Ms. Consuela was the first person to spot me. "Albert!!" she said. You came back! We were all so worried about you!" She wrapped her arms around me, and I could feel the love and concern she felt. Soon, everyone heard the commotion, and the hallway was filled with all my friends and the other counselors. Everyone welcomed me back and was glad that I had returned.

Mr. Thomas made his way through the crowd. I could see that he had a stern look on his face. It was almost like the one my father would have when he was tired of me. "Well, it's about time you showed up," he said. I could hear the disappointment in his voice. I avoided looking into his eyes, but I could feel them bearing down on me. "You've caused so much trouble around here, I thought we might have to close down."

"Sorry," was all I could get out.

"Look at me," he said. His voice was low and booming.

I forced myself to look into his blue eyes. I could see the disappointment, but I could also see that he cared. His brow was furrowed, and his arms were crossed, but he didn't seem mad. The emotion I read from him was relief. Still, I had to turn my head to keep from crying.

"Why'd you do it?" he said.

I shrugged. I couldn't come up with a good answer. "I just had to get out." "Well, you coulda ended up back in prison. Do you want that?"

"No sir," I said.

"I should throw you in there because your absence has affected the entire program. I don't think the sun shined bright while you weren't here. Hell, Morris hasn't listened to a thing I've said since you left."

I spotted my friend among the crowd of people surrounding me. I could tell he was holding back tears, and I was happy to see him.

I looked around the room. "I'm sorry, everyone." I managed to croak out. "It's okay," some of them said.

"You're back now."

"Things can finally get back to normal."

Things did get back to normal. I went back to helping Ms. Consuela in the kitchen. Mr. Thomas kept an even closer watch on me to ensure I didn't leave again. I continued with my education,  Tony and I remained close. The months seemed to fly by, and I was released back into the world before I knew it. I would be free to do what I wanted without anyone's guidance.

"Hey, Hampton!" Mr. Thomas said to me one day. "I got some good news for ya!"

"Yes, sir," I said.

"We've been thinking, and we want you to stay on with us." "You want my sentence to be longer?" My heart sank.

"No, not like that," Mr. Thomas continued. "We want you to stay on as a mentor to the kids who come in. We will pay you and give you a place to stay. What do you think about that?"

I couldn't think. My mind was swimming. I did love being at ACI, and it did have a profound effect on me, but I missed home. Since escaping, I hadn't seen my little brother and missed my family in Fort Lauderdale. So, after I thought it over, I decided to return home. I sometimes think about how my life would have been different if I had chosen to stay at ACI and become a counselor. This would probably be the shortest story ever with a happy ending, but I didn't make that decision. I turned down the offer and went home. I promised Mr. Thomas that I would finish school and keep my life on track. If only our promises were as easy to maintain as they are to say. I was released from ACI on March 9, 1973, and I was back home that same day. I was finishing school and enjoying being with my family, but the light that ACI had put in me dimmed as soon as I got home. I didn't want to be at my parents' house that long. I could feel the urge to return to the streets, and I was broke.

I had never been so broke in my life. I was making money from the time I was eight, so not having a dime to my name was enough to drive me crazy. I had to do something to get some money, and fast. That would calm my mind down.

So, I had the bright idea of robbing a gas station. On March 10, 1973, I walked into a local gas station and tried to rob them. It was my bad luck that this particular gas station had been robbed twice recently, and the police were now staking it out, looking for anyone else who might try to do the same. I didn't have a gun with me, but the courts called it "strong-armed robbery."

I was so ashamed that the news might return to ACI, and it did. Mr. Thomas, his wife, Ms. Consuela, and all the other program members were so disappointed. What made it worse was that they couldn't have me back. Stealing from a school when no one is there is different from stealing from a convenience store while people are there. Since ACI was a community-based program, they couldn't have a hardened criminal like me back in the community. So, ACI was out.

I was sent to Okeechobee School for Boys this time, and there was no ACI. We had bars on our windows, lockdown, uniforms, and guards.

We were not members of a program but inmates. I didn't feel the sense of brotherhood I felt at ACI. I felt the need for survival. My old ways of fighting quickly returned while I was there. I ended up beating a boy up the first night I was there because he told one of the guards I was smoking a joint. I was smoking, but it was none of his business what I was doing, but I knew it was.

They had a pool table there, and I took full advantage of it. I was taking those boys for all their commissary. My love for the game hadn't died, and my skills hadn't slackened. I discovered that the guards even placed bets on some of my games. I made some deals to get a cut of that money as well.

As I continued at Okeechobee, Mr. Thomas and all I learned at ACI became further from my memory. The street life was calling me, and I was determined to return there. From March until November 15, 1973, my life was a cycle of violence. I was either about to fight somebody or fighting somebody almost every day. They might have thrown a party when I finally returned to the streets.

# Chapter 4

There is a saying that people use when they love the fast life of the city. They say, "The streets are calling me." People don't take this seriously. They know that the streets can't talk, and the person who is saying it is just addicted to a fast lifestyle. I would beg to differ from them. I believe that the streets can talk just as well as anyone else. There's a voice, a heartbeat, a rhythm, and a cadence only certain people can hear. Like any vice, the streets talk to people, and back then, I chose to listen.

After I left Okeechobee School for Boys, I found my way back to 27th Ave. I jumped right back into place like I never left. I knew the mistakes I made last time and wouldn't repeat them; no hard drugs or anything that could cloud my mind. That meant heroin was out. I never touched the stuff again. I did pick up a little cocaine habit, but I had it under control. I kept my circle small, and I stayed away from the law.

I went back to playing pool at Hick's, so I could make some quick money. Some of the same people were there but also new faces. Some people from over in Miami started hanging around and had connections with prominent people in Miami. So, I made it my business to talk to them and get in their good graces. A friendly pool game can put anyone at ease, especially if you let them win a few times. My new friends introduced me to their friends, and I now had connections with their friends.

I met and mingled with names that would eventually become infamous in Miami and worldwide. They gave me drugs to sell, and we both made money. I was on my way to becoming a kingpin. People would look up to me, and I wouldn't run just 27th Ave, but Florida. 1974 was a blockbuster year for me. Many of my high school graduating class had made it to college, and many decided to return to my old stomping grounds. In Daytona, there was an HBCU, which means Historically Black College or University. Many of my friends decided to go to Bethune-Cookman College. Since I had missed out on so much of their high school life, I decided that's where I wanted to be.

The college girls had my attention. There were girls from all across America: tall, short, light, dark, and I was right there. I had the best clothes, flashy jewelry, and a 1973 Cadillac Fleetwood. My car was so friendly people would wave me down at the traffic light and compliment me. I got it from this widowed woman who never drove it. So, it was new and got me the right kind of attention. If my clothes and cars didn't get the girls, what I was selling brought them the rest of the way.

Methaqualone is a drug designed in the 1950s to help fight malaria. It is a sedative that helps put people to sleep. Over the years, people have found that if they take the proper dosage of the drug, they don't go to sleep, but they can calm down and focus. It made them feel like their brains were operating on a higher level. So, by the 1970s, Methaqualone now had street names like "disco biscuits," but most people just called them by their brand name, Quaaludes.

The girls at BCC loved Quaaludes. They said it helped them study and pass their tests. Either way, it helped me and them. I went to talk to pretty girls; they got good grades, and I got paid. It was a win for everyone, but I always came out on top. I rode the road between Fort Lauderdale and Daytona Beach every weekend for almost a year. I always went back home with more money and less drugs.

I had a few rules that I kept to so the police would stay off my trail. I always made sure my car was in top working order. Oil changes, tires, lights, and even the car wash were frequent stops for me. Being broken down on the side of the road could make some officers pull over to help me, and they could become suspicious. I always drove the speed limit. The road could be empty, and my car would not go faster than the posted sign. I just knew that's when an officer would be hidden in a cut somewhere, waiting to pull somebody over. I also never went by myself. I needed someone to have my back in case I got jammed up. Even Lump went with me a couple of times.

I would sometimes drive by the ACI building and look at the kids participating in the program now. I remember a few short years ago that I was me, and the people who worked there probably had the same hopes for them as they did for me. I would spot Mr. Thomas sometimes in the windows or walking the grounds. I wanted to stop my car, walk up to him and apologize for not taking him up on his offer, but I was too ashamed. I wasn't living right then, so those words would mean nothing coming from me, and I wasn't ready to stop and do anything different. The money was too good.

I made over two hundred thousand dollars in 1974. It was a good year. I could care for myself and help the rest of my family out. I had a nice car, a nice place to stay, and the best clothes that money could buy. 1975 was an even better year. That year, I made close to seven hundred thousand dollars. I was living the dream. I traveled the entire state of Florida doing whatever I wanted. Concerts, fashion shows, and women were nothing for me. I went from seeing James Brown in concert, sitting at a South Beach fashion show, and partying at the Limelight all in one weekend.

I saw so much of Florida that I jumped at the chance when an uncle of mine invited me on a trip to New York. Ever since I met Nut all those years ago, I had always wanted to go, and he would tell us country boys how it was in the big city. My uncle was preparing to deploy with the U.S. Army and wanted me to join him for a trip.

Miami is a big city but a country town compared to New York. When they say it is the city that never sleeps, they mean it. You could tell I was a tourist because I walked around with my head up in the air the whole time. For miles, all you can see is skyscrapers and people. And since I was a tourist, I didn't mind acting like one. I rode the subway to landmarks like the Empire State Building and the Twin Towers. I tried the food and walked around Times Square. That was when it was so family-friendly that you would likely see anything down there.

When Nut found out I was in town, he couldn't wait to show me around. "You country niggas done made it to the Big Apple!" he said when I greeted him.

"Yeah!" I said. "So make sure you show us a good time."

And that he did. Nut took us all over the city and then some. They say it's the city that never sleeps, and they were right. There was always a party or a club to go to, and we didn't make it in most nights until well into the morning. I almost became nocturnal the way I would be up at night and sleeping during the day. I was in love with New York and didn't want to leave. I even called myself finding a girl up there, but she was in the service and deployed with my uncle. I never saw her again.

Those two years were magical to me. Even though I was dealing drugs and having to look out for the police, I didn't think life could get any better.

I was still on probation for my previous incarceration, and I had to get a job. It was funny because no job I could find around Fort Lauderdale paid me a fraction of what I was making on the streets, but I had to keep the police from looking into what I was doing, so I got a job.

In 1976, the BETA program helped people on probation get jobs, and I was one of them. A man named Frenchie hired me to work with the City of Sunrise. I would ride around the city and do maintenance, like fixing light poles, filling in potholes, and other tasks. I liked the people I worked with well enough, and it gave me something different to do. The work was honest.

I was only supposed to work there for three months, so I didn't mind the work. There was this white boy with whom I worked and had a good relationship. If he were going to the store, I would bring something back and vice versa. One day, he asked me if I wanted something from the store, and I gave him money for a soda. When he returned from the store, I asked for my change, and he said, "Ain't no change." I don't know, but something about how he said that about my money got me into a rage. I hauled off and punched him dead in his mouth. He looked shocked, and so did I.

When I looked down at my hand, I saw that his front teeth were stuck in my knuckles, and he was bleeding. The fight was broken up after that, and Frenchie pulled me to the side.

"Now come on, Hampton," he said. He had the disappointed look that I had come to know too well. "You can't be doing shit like that. Do you know who his daddy is?"

"I don't care!" I said. I was ready for another round.

"His daddy is over this program, man," he said. "Calm down before you ruin this good thing."

I calmed down, Frenchie smoothed over the fight, and I could keep my job.

A couple weeks after the fight, it was the Fourth of July. I decided to take my day off from the City of Sunrise to go play some pool down at Hick's. I had been running so much that I forgot how much I loved 27th Ave and how much I loved playing pool. So, it was a nice, sunny, and hot day in Fort Lauderdale.

It was like old times when I was younger, with Chocolate running the room and I was playing on a table in the back. After some time, a little cousin, who we nicknamed Red, and a friend from my neighborhood came in for a game. I said hello and went back to practicing my game.

After a while, I heard a commotion coming from their table. Something had gone wrong during their game, and they had started fighting. I went over to them to see what was wrong. "What are y'all doing?" I said when I was able to get them apart. "Cut this shit out!" They calmed down and started playing again. After a little while, they started fighting again. This time, I decided that I would take it a step further. I went over and hit Red and the boy over the head with my pistol. Red stopped, but my childhood friend took it a step further. He ran off and said he would return with his father to settle the score.

"I think you need to leave, man said Mr. Snow from the barbershop next door, he had heard about the commotion and came over to calm things down.

"I ain't goin' nowhere!" I said. I was defiant and wouldn't be moved.

Mr. Snow sighed and said, "Okay." He headed back to his shop, knowing that things would get worse. In hindsight, I should have listened to him and left right then, but you know what they say about hindsight.

I returned to the pool and left my gun in one of the ball racks. After a little while, my old friend and his father walked in. I remembered Mr. Gregg from the neighborhood when I was growing up. I even used to cut his yard when I was younger, and I thought I would be able to reason with him.

I stood up and put my hand on my gun. Mr. Gregg stood on the long end of the pool table with his son looking over his shoulder at me like the little kid he was. I can almost remember him saying, "There he is, Daddy. That's the nigga who hit me with the gun."

"What's going on, son?" Mr. Gregg said.

"Nothing much, sir," I said. "Just playing some pool." "Well, my son told me y'all got to fighting up here."

"Your son told a lie. I was fighting nobody. He and my cousin fought, and I had to break them up twice."

"You had to hit him with a gun, though?"

My hand tightened around my gun. "I had to get them niggas' attention. They wouldn't listen to reason."

"I think you coulda found a better way than that."

"I broke em' up without it, and they started again, so I hit em' with the gun. Do you see em' fighting now?"

A couple of people laughed who were listening in.

"Man!" the son interjected from behind his father. "That nigga just talking that shit because he got that gun. I promise when I catch you without it, that's yo ass nigga!"

I looked at my cousin and handed him my gun. "You ain't said nothin', nigga! I'm right here."

I forgot that Mr. Gregg, Chocolate, Red, and anyone else was there, so I jumped on him. I punched him in the mouth, slammed him on the floor, and started beating him in the head. I let loose on him like he was owed this ass-whooping for a long time.

Then, all of a sudden, I felt a sharp pain in my head, and my vision became blurry. I felt like I was going to pass out. Mr. Gregg had taken one of the pool cues and cracked me over the head. Blood was starting to run down my face and blur my vision even more.

"Give me my gun!" I yelled to Red.

Mr. Gregg tried to swing at him but missed. My cousin was able to get the gun into my hand, and I was able to shoot. I shot Mr. Gregg four times, and I tried to shoot his son, but he took off running. That was the only thing that saved his life.

When I stood up, the world almost went black. I was stumbling and trying to stay awake. Most of the world looked red because of the blood that covered my vision.

"Come on, man," Chocolate said to me. "We gotta go to the hospital. You are not looking too good."

I went down and got in Chocolate's car, and the ride to the hospital felt like it took forever. I was fading in and out of consciousness, trying to hold on to reality. My short life was flashing before my eyes, and all I could think of was how many things there were still left for me to do. I must have passed out between getting to the hospital and surgery because I don't remember anything.

What I do remember is waking up handcuffed to the hospital bed. I was under arrest for assault and possessing a weapon as a felon.

# Chapter 5

If I didn't have a gun, I would have never seen the inside of a jail cell. If I had taken that pool stick and beat Mr. Gregg in the head like he did me, I would have gotten out of the hospital and gone home.

No, I had to have a gun in my possession and be a felon at the same time. Because It was self-defense. A father and son were jumping me, and Mr. Gregg walloped me in the head. I could have died. He would be the one in this jail getting this nasty food.

Mr. Gregg was paralyzed. He would have limited use of his body below his neck for the rest of his life. His son, who ran, had escaped and was only alive because my vision was so hazy from being hit in the head with the pool cue. Sitting in my cell, I thought about how my life had changed in such a short time. I was about to be on probation. I was making more money than my parents or grandparents could imagine. I was sitting in the front row of fashion shows, and now I was waiting in line to receive the nasty food they give people in jail, wearing one of those ugly orange jumpsuits. I didn't know who to blame, but I was angry.

I should have minded my business and let my cousin fight that boy. They would have probably made up. It was just a game of pool, but I had seen games of pool get out of control when money was involved. My gun wasn't the first one to fire inside of Hick's, but I knew better. I wasn't supposed to see the inside of these walls ever again.

I had to see my mother's crying face again in the visitor's area. I had to see my father looking at me with that same disappointment. I had to think of Mr. Thomas back at ACI and how I had failed him and everyone in the program.

I couldn't get over the fact that I was trying to keep my cousin or friend from seeing the inside of these walls, and I found myself there.

I would have nightmares about Mr. Gregg at night. I was back on 14th Ct. I was cutting his yard again like I did when I was eight. He would come out and wave and tell me good job. When I would look up to say thank you, I would see him lying on the ground, blood pooling around his body, and a gun in my hand. I would pop up on my bed in a cold sweat. I'd look around my cell and get mad all over again. I was missing everything while I was trapped in these walls. I could feel my connections drying up, my money drying up, and my life drying up.

My lawyer came to visit me. He said he could get me out for a three-year stint in prison. I wasn't about to do that. In three years, the entire world could be different. The street life was fast, and nothing stayed the same. In three years, your whole crew and connections could be gone with a new regime in their place and running things. I told him to go back and renegotiate it. He came back with twenty-one months. It wasn't ideal, but it was better than spending three years locked down. At least with that, I could get good behavior and be out in about a year.

My first stop was the River Junction Correctional Facility in Chattahoochee, FL. I didn't stay there long before I was shipped off to the Jacksonville Vocational Center. This would be the place where most of my sentence would be served. It was a small camp. There couldn't have been more than seventy inmates in the facility, and they had decent food.

Anyone unlucky enough to get sent to JVC would have to put up with the meanest warden ever. Even the other guards would scurry away when this man came around. His name was Lee Forrest Harris, and he had a permanent chip on his shoulder. He looked like what they told us was supposed to be a "good guy," but he was anything but that. He had blonde hair and blue eyes. He may as well have been daring people to look at those eyes so that he could find a punishment for you. He was a medium-weight man who walked upright as if he always had somewhere to go, and he was the most important person in the room.

This wasn't my first run-in with Warden Harris, though. He was one of the counselors at ACI when I was there six years prior. I had no direct contact with him; Mr. Thomas ensured he was my main counselor, but I remember seeing Mr. Harris around. He seemed like a nice enough dude, like the other counselors. The only thing that made him stand out was his bright blonde hair and those sharp blue eyes. I wondered why he was here and why he had not moved up the ranks of ACI until I got to know him.

I don't think I ever heard Warden Harris say, "Good morning!" to anyone. His first words were a command, and everything that followed was either a threat or an insult. One day, a guard found himself a little too happy. It might have been his anniversary, his wife may have found out she was pregnant, or it may have been his birthday. Whatever it was, it had him in a particularly happy mood.

It wasn't like he was letting inmates get away with anything or causing a distraction; he was just happy. Warden Harris couldn't have that. He called the officer out in front of the whole camp.

"The hell is wrong with you?" Warden Harris said as he approached the guard.

The guard looked confused, and his smile quickly faded. "Me, sir?" He pointed to himself.

"No, I'm talking to the other jackass smiling like the damn Cheshire cat!" Warden Harris said.

"I'm sorry, sir. I didn't mean…"

"You didn't mean what? To be out here looking like a damn fool in front of everyone?" The entire camp fell silent as everyone's attention turned toward the two. "What's got you in such a good mood this morning? You win the lottery or something?"

"No, sir. I just…"

"Oh, I know. You got a little boyfriend out here, and he did somethin' to make you feel good. Is that it? You got one of these boys to put that smile on your face?"

"No, sir!" the guard responded. Any resemblance of a smile he once had was gone. The guard's face seemed to be changing colors right before our eyes. He started pale, then pink, and finally a bright red.

"Yeah, that's it." Warden Harris said. "These boys got you hot under the collar, huh?" He started to circle the guard like a shark in the water. "You bout to burst? These boys got you so hot."

"No, sir!" The guard said. All the light in his eyes was gone.

"Then I don't wanna see you with a grin like that around here anymore. Or else I'm gonna lock you in a cell with one of the big boys overnight. Am I understood?"

"Yes, sir!" the guard responded.

Warden Harris walked away with a devilish smile on his face. Those would be the only times he would smile. That devil would show his grin when he felt like he broke you down.

That officer wasn't the same anymore. He wasn't overly friendly, to begin with, but now he was a little colder and sterner to us inmates. Instead of telling us not to do something, he now barked it. He hardly ever smiled again, but when he did, he ensured that Warden Harris wasn't around.

Warden Harris somehow managed to find a woman who would call herself his wife. She looked like she was a lovely enough lady. Like him, she had blonde hair and blue eyes. She was slender and was nice looking. So, for the life of everyone on the camp, we couldn't figure out why she was married to a monster. He didn't even seem to treat her that well. He would sometimes come to the camp with her in the car and make her sit there all day. She wouldn't get out, go to the bathroom, or even get a drink of water. She would be in the car all day. The air conditioner wouldn't be on, the car wouldn't be running, and the windows were up most of the time. I know people go to jail for doing their pets like that; it has to be against the law to do that to your wife. Still, I never saw her complain or say much of anything. Most of us thought she must have been a little off to put up with that foolishness, but it wasn't like we could ask her. The inmates were forbidden to talk to anyone outside the gates, and the guards were too afraid of Warden Harris.

Warden Harris was also a thicf. We used to do trustee work in the community, like I did with the BETA program. They would have us digging ditches, clearing land for construction, and landscaping. The work was hard, but it wasn't anything that I wasn't used to. Warren Harris would go out with us on some of these trips. He had plans for public office in Jacksonville and would use us to work around the community to boost his public image. In front of those cameras, he was a different person. He was friendly and personable and almost came off like a natural person. If those people only knew how he was behind closed doors, they'd say he needed to be out there with us.

Some days, we worked a job, and Warden Harris would tell us to put the equipment that didn't belong to JVC in the back of the truck. Some of the guys did it, but I wasn't crazy. I knew that if we got caught taking anything from the site, that snake would turn on us and have us all with longer sentences. So, I always put whatever I was working with back where I got it. There was this farm down the road from the camp that had cows.

Sometimes, those cows would graze too far from the herd, and Warden Harris would be waiting. He would get a couple of guys out of their cells and have them on patrol at night for a rogue cow that got a little too close to the fence and have them slaughter it.

There would be steak and meat for days. Remember, I did say the food was good. I don't know if the farmers ever said anything about their missing livestock, but I don't think they were that stupid not to notice something was up.

I tried my best to stay out of the warden's way. I kept my head down because I was determined not to spend a day over the twenty-one months I had been sentenced. I did an excellent job of it until he spotted me in the yard one day.

One of my fellow inmates was a karate expert. He had a black belt and was a champion like I was in pool. He was in prison for almost beating someone to death over a bet. During rec time, he gave some other inmates a class, showing us some basic moves. I was one of those students and enjoyed learning the moves. Plus, it was good exercise. Well, Warden Harris couldn't have that.

"Are you showing these inmates how to fight?" he said as he stormed over to where we were practicing. The inmate looked down to avoid his gaze. "It looks to me like you're training them for battle, am I right?"

"No, sir," the inmate responded. "It's just some basic moves for exercise."
"Well, cut that shit out. I don't want anyone getting any ideas around here."

"Yes, sir," he responded. And that was the end of karate classes for about a week. Warden Harris got sick and was out for another two weeks. God must have smiled at us, so we continued practicing karate.

As luck would have it, Warden Harris would get better and return during rec time one day. We were in the corner doing our basic moves when he started screaming from the other side of the yard. "Didn't I tell y'all about doing that damn karate? He was marching over to us. His face was red, and his eyes looked like they were bulging. "I swear, If brains were a disease y' all wouldn't get sick."

Everything in my head told me to shut up and just take it. He called us everything but a child of God, and we were all just taking it. We were felons, sure, but we were still grown men who deserved to be treated like grown men. "Aw, man!" I shouted, "We are just out here exercising. Ain't nobody gettin' hurt by this."

It was almost like a switch went off because he immediately stopped focusing on our karate instructor and looked right at me. "You said something?" I could see the rage growing in his eyes. Nobody talked back to him or disobeyed him.

"We ain't hurtin' nobody," I repeated slowly, emphasizing that I was talking to him.

"Well, you goin' to jail!" he replied.

"What?" I asked, looking confused. I looked around to see other confused faces in the crowd.

The yard was dead silent. The other guards didn't even move. I don't think the wind was even blowing. He was like a firecracker, ready to explode.

"Get in my office!" He said through gritted teeth.

The other inmates looked at me like I had just signed my death certificate. No one ever wanted to go to Warden Harris's office. It almost became a legend about what would happen if you went in there. I heard everything from being killed and your body being sold off to science or being transferred to maximum security. Either way, I was about to find out.

I held my head high as I walked toward the building. I walked down the hallway to the door that had Warden Lee Harris. I knew that whatever was waiting for me on the other side of that door would change how I walked around this camp until I got out.

Walking into the small office, I took time to take in my surroundings. He had a dark brown desk made of heavy wood. I guessed that he must have stolen it. Two dark blue chairs faced the desk, and a big brown chair was for him. On the desk, he had pictures of his family. These people looked like they loved him or they were good pretenders. He even had a picture of him and his wife on the desk. The woman in the photo looked different from the sad, tired, and hot woman he made sit in the car all day. On the walls, he had newspaper articles run by journalists ignorant of what he was really like. Headlines Like "Harris Eyes Public Office," "Harris Makes Crime Work for Us," and "The Program at JVC Produces Results." The articles were accompanied by pictures of him with that fake smile. It was almost enough to make me sick. If they only knew the man we had to deal with every day, they might write something like "The Devil is a Warden" or "Psychopath, Thief, and Monster: The Real Warden Harris."

The door slammed behind me as I was looking around the room. "Just who do you think you are, boy?!" Warden Harris said. He bumped into me as he went around his desk. "You have some kinda nerve speakin' like that to me in front of all those people like that."

I tried to keep my mouth shut, but it was building up inside me like a volcano. "All this about some exercise?" I blurted out. I thought I might explode if I kept it in.

"You're dumber than you look, and that is saying somethin," he snarled at me from behind his desk. "Looks like you need a little time by yourself to get your mind right."

My stomach dropped. He was about to put me in the basement of the building, otherwise known as solitary confinement. He was good at that. I would have preferred if he tried to beat me or something. I've heard stories from other inmates about what it was like down there. It was always damp, and you were going to get sick. You had no contact with anyone other than the guard who brought you your food, the mattress on the cot was old and smelled of mold, and the only window only got slight sunlight for about 30 minutes a day.

Warden Harris fumbled at his desk and got some and a pair of handcuffs. My heart started racing. He walked around the desk and reached for my arm. I snatched it back and moved out of the way. I could feel the heat coming off him; he was so mad. He went for it again, and this time he grabbed me. I pushed him, but he still held my arm, so we started struggling. We knocked over the two chairs facing his desk, and some of his pictures shifted. Warden Harris tried to get me in a chokehold, but I wiggled out of it. I pushed him hard, and he slammed against the wall behind his desk. The pictures with the fake headlines fell and shattered on the floor, and his watch broke.

"Now, you've done it, nigger!" he said to me through gritted teeth. He reached into his desk again, and the light caught the shine on the gleam of a pistol. This man was going to shoot and kill me, and there was nothing anyone could do about it.

I turned toward the door and ran out. I ran past the receptionist and out the front door of the camp. I knew he was in my tracks and could hear him running down the hallway.

"Get your black ass back here, goddammit!" he yelled after me.

I looked around and tried to figure out what I would do next. I had nowhere to run and no one to run to. Luckily, there were some men across the street at a fire station. Other than Warden Harris probably stealing tools from them, they had no connection to the man. So, they would have no reason to be afraid of him.

I could still hear him after me. "Get back here!" he roared.

"Aye!" I yelled out. Some of the firefighters looked in my direction. "Y'all see this man out here trying to kill me?" I pointed at Warden Harris, who had just made his way outside. "I don't have a weapon, and he's trying to kill me!" I had everyone on the site's full attention now.

Warden Harris was even madder than before. He tried to conceal his gun before anyone could see him. "Get your ass over here, Hampton!"

"He has a gun!" I yelled to keep everyone looking.

By this time, the other guards in the camp had come out to help get me back inside. I felt safer now because even though they were afraid of him, I don't think they would take it too lightly if he killed someone in front of them. Even he wouldn't want to have to explain shooting an inmate while he was running for office. It would break the persona of a good man he had put out. So, I surrendered and was led back inside by the guards.

When we got back to his office, Warden Harris laid into me. "That little stunt you pulled was cute, real cute!" He said. He paced back and forth while four guards surrounded me. "Whatever time you thought you were gonna get, you can count it doubled."

I wanted to scream out, but I could be facing more charges for assaulting an officer and possibly escaping, so I would take more time in solitary than more time in prison altogether.

I let the other officers handcuff me. I was glad that Harris wouldn't get the satisfaction of putting the cuffs on me. However, even though I was cuffed and about to be left in solitary, he couldn't help but try to get one last hit in. He took the butt of the gun and tried to hit me over the head with it. It was November, so it was cold outside, and I was wearing a beanie that was sticking up a little higher than my head. So, when I ducked, he missed my head and knocked my cap off. This made him even madder. I thought his entire face and neck would explode.

"Get this piece of shit out of my face!" he said through gritted teeth.

The guards marched me to the elevator, which would take me to the bottom floor of the camp. I could feel the light dimming as we passed each floor. When we reached the bottom, I could smell the dampness. The walls looked like they were slick with sweat and pain. The guards led me to my cell, uncuffed me, and locked the door behind me.

I took some time to take in my surroundings and adjust my eyes to the room's darkness. The other inmates did not lie when they said this place was terrible. The mattress was old and ratty, with stains from the previous tenants of Solitary, and that little window let in the faintest ray of light into the room.

I sat down on the musty cot and thought about how long I would be there. I must have been sitting there for hours, but it felt like days. It gave me time to think about that day's events and how I was even more troubled. When you're in solitary, you get nothing.

You don't get phone calls or visits to see the sun. It would be me and thought inside my head for however long the warden saw fit.

"Hampton!" I heard a voice say. I sat up straight and looked around. "Hampton! You up in there?"

"Yeah, I'm up," I said.

"Dinner time." I heard the man say. He opened the small window on the door and slid the tray in.

"At least the food is good," I thought as I slid the tray out the window. I looked over my food and noticed a pack of cookies that would only be available in the commissary was sitting on my tray. I looked at the package strangely and wondered why I would get this type of food when I had just been placed in solitary.

"Hey," I heard the guard say. "I heard you put Harris on his ass today." The man let out a laugh.

"Yeah," I replied with a chuckle. "Got me in here, though."

"Bout time someone put him in his place. He's walking around here like he owns the place. A waste of man and say he wanna be somebody's senator." The man kissed his teeth.

"Do you know how long I got in here?"

"I heard them say something about two months."

I sighed deeply. It was long, but it could have been worse. What I did could have added years onto my sentence.

"Hey," I heard the guard say. "Do this time, but don't let this time do you. I've seen people go crazy down here." "Yes, sir," I responded.

"I got something else for you," he said. He opened the window on the cell door and slid in a book.

I left my tray of food on my cot to pick it up. It was an old Bible. The pages were worn with age, and I could tell whoever owned this Bible had done some serious reading.

"Thank you," I said as I took the book and went to sit back down.

"No problem," he replied. "You have to keep your mind focused so you don't go crazy down here, and you don't have to be in a building like this again for the rest of your life."

"Yeah. This is gonna be my last trip to prison."

"That's the right kinda attitude to have. Now, finish that dinner so I can return the tray."

I ate my food and gave the guard the tray back. He left me with some encouragement, and I lay on the musty cot that would be my bed for the next two months. The cell in solitary was cold, and it didn't make it any better due to the fact November had just begun. I would be in that cell for the coldest months of the year. I wouldn't even be able to hear my parents say Merry Christmas, and I would probably only get the scraps off of whatever cow Warden Harris had the boys to slaughter around that time. All I could do to keep my mind off it was read the Bible the guard left me.

I started with Genesis and read about how God created the world and how the people he created did their best to mess everything up. It wasn't too far off from how people acted in the present. I read about all the people, the hate, the crime, and the wars and thought about how little people have changed since the beginning of time. We struggle to make a way on this rock God put us on.

I spent the rest of my time working out. I would do sets of push-ups, sit-ups, and jumping jacks in the morning when I woke up, around lunchtime, and before dinner. It was an excellent way to keep me warm and keep track of the day.

The guard, who I came to know as Reggie, came and talked to me from time to time. He would tell me stories about his wife and how they had been married for fifteen years. They had two children, and he wanted to find a new line of work.

I told him he needed to stay in this line of work because he seemed to care about the inmates. He reminded me of Mr. Thomas from ACI, a person who cared. He would bring me extra food and some baked goods from his wife. We'd sit and talk while he was on shift, and I would tell him stories about my crazy life.

"Why didn't you keep playing pool?" he asked one day.

"I still play when I have time," I said. "Life just got in the way." "You could have made some good money if you went pro."

"I know; I just got caught up doing things I shouldn't have." "It's never too late to turn it around."

The two months in solitary confinement seemed to fly past from reading the Bible, talking to Reggie, and working out. So, when Harris decided I would get out, it was almost like another day. The main difference was the fresh air and direct sunlight. The first thing they did was send me to the doctor to make sure I didn't get too sick down there and pass something to the other inmates.

After talking with the doctor and informing him of my history of asthma and how the dampness affected my breathing while in solitary, I couldn't do hard labor, so I was assigned to work on the inside of the building.

My new office duties pissed Warden Harris off tremendously. "You can't work outside?"

"My asthma messes with me I said."

He crumpled up the note from the doctor. "Hell no. I'm going to have to get your black ass out of here. I don't need another custodian. I need people working outside. You must find a new camp if you can't do that."

"The doctor said it, not me," I added.

"I don't care what he said. You weren't too sick to be outside doing karate and playing softball. Now, you're too ill to work outside. That's bullshit, and you know it."

For the next few weeks, Warden Harris would remind me that he was having me transferred to another camp. He didn't have any use for me if he couldn't parade me in front of cameras for his political career. I heard him, but I didn't pay him any mind. I swept and mopped the floors and maintained a friendly relationship with Reggie.

One morning, the door to my cell opened. "Pack it up, Hampton," I heard the guard say. Warden Haris had done it. I was being transferred out of JVC to another camp. Warden Harris made sure to be at the van while I was leaving. His blue eyes looked straight at me, and he had a devilish grin. "Well, Hampton," he said. He looked like he was about to explode with laughter. "It looks like you're not JVC material. We just couldn't help you here. Maybe this new camp would accommodate somebody with all your ailments more."

I didn't say anything. I wouldn't give him the satisfaction of knowing he had the last laugh, but my stomach was in knots. I knew it would be hell if he had anything to do with my transfer location. He would probably try to send me to a maximum security prison where the guards pissed in the food before they handed it out.

I stepped into the van without a word and headed to my next location.

I was returned to River Junction for a few days before being sent to the West Chapter of ACI. I was initially excited because I remember how great it was in the teen program, but I was greatly disappointed. This was different from the program in Daytona. Those were boys, but these were grown men, and we had none of the freedoms we had in Daytona. We were not participants in a program, but we were inmates in prison.

There was no speaking to kids, planting gardens, or helping in the kitchen. I didn't have a Mr. Thomas watching my back. All I had was guards barking orders at me, nasty food, and a rundown cot to sleep on. I was so happy that I was only there for a few weeks before I got transferred to work release. Work release was much better than the last camps I went to. As the name said, we had jobs. We worked in the community but had to return to the camp at night. We had much more freedom, and the supervisors didn't breathe down our necks like the guards.

The other inmates in the program were cool as well. I met a man named Carl who was from the country town of Ocala. Carl had on some of the most excellent shoes I had ever seen. I told him about my friend Big Man from Ocala and how he talked about how country it was.

"It is country," Carl said. "But we got somehtin' goin' there. You should come visit when you get out."

"I don't know about that," I said. "I'm a city boy, and I don't have nothin' to do with Mayberry."

"Well, that's where I'm headed today. And I can't wait."

Carl went home to Ocala that day, and I finished serving my time in the work release program.

I was released on March 31, 1978, and I could hear the old call of the streets in my ear, and it was like I had never left.`

# Chapter 6

I was ready to return to business when my feet hit the pavement in Fort Lauderdale. As I suspected, the streets had gotten hold of some of my connections. The Feds, the streets, the drugs, and the life still happened when I was locked down. I was upset but not deterred. Going back to 27th Ave would get me back on track, and I would be better. I knew this time I wouldn't let anything send me back to prison.

My cousin Red, who was in the fight at the pool hall, started selling some weed for me. He felt terrible that he was the reason I was locked down for twenty-one months. He wouldn't take any money from me for any of the weed he sold. It was the least he could do to pay me back.

Red and I became close when I got out of prison. Not only was he selling the drugs for me, we used to hang out a lot. One of our stomping grounds was the 19th St Park. We would go and play basketball, shoot dice, and sell some weed while we were there. That's where I met a lifelong friend with the nickname Small Fry. He was younger than Red and I, and he had the name Small Fry for a reason. He was shorter than me, and I was not tall myself.

One day, while Red, Small Fry, and I were playing basketball at the park, we met someone who would change our lives. His name was John Harris, and he was from Ocala, FL. Something about Ocala just kept popping back up in my life. Big Man was from Ocala, Carl was from Ocala, and now John is from Ocala.

"I didn't know it was that many niggas in Ocala," I said. "Thought it was just a bunch of horse farms and shit up there."

"Nah, man," John said with a laugh. "It is a lot of horses, but it's black folks up there. But what's there is some money. Y'all think y'all cleaning up around here, just come to Ocala, and it'll blow your mind."

I was still on the fence about going to Ocala. I didn't know anyone there. I think Big Man had moved back, and Carl was out by now, but I didn't want to chance going somewhere and getting pinched in another county. The police had to be racist up there. I just knew it.

However, Small Fry and Red were sold. They heard that Ocala was where the real money was, so they needed to be there.

"Y'all done let that country nigga come down here and convince you that's where you need to be?"

"The worst that can happen is that we don't make any money," Fry said. "Right," Red added. "If we don't make nothin' in Ocala, we'll just come home and sell it here."

"No, that's not the worst thing that could happen," I said. "You could get pinched up there and end up in one of the country ass jails, or y'all green asses could be swingin' from a tree like some strange fruit."

"Aw," Fry said, "I know you ain't scared." "Nah, nigga. I ain't stupid."

"Don't even say stuff like that," Red said. "We're gonna do good there."

I ended up getting aggravated with both of them and gave in. I would give them some weed to go to Ocala for the weekend. I made sure to let them know that I would put some money on their books when they got locked up. Fry and Red left on Friday for Ocala. I couldn't help but worry about both of them. They were my little cousin and my new best friend. They were

so young, though, and I didn't want anything bad to happen to them.

Early Saturday morning, around two o'clock, my phone started ringing. I just knew that someone was calling from jail or telling me that something bad had happened to them. I gathered myself before I answered the phone.

"Hello," I said hesitantly. "Cicero!" Red said urgently.

"What?" I said. My heart started beating out of my chest. "You not gonna believe this!"

"What? Where's Fry?" "He's alright," Red said.

I calmed down some. "What's happening?" "You ain't gonna believe this!"

"Say what you need to say!" I was overly aggravated now. "We sold out!" "Huh?"

"You heard me; everything you gave us is gone. We sold out!" "That fast?"

"Hell, yeah! The weed these country niggas got up here may as well be hay. We had repeat customers up here already, and they are returning for more."

"Well, damn." is all I could say. They were right, and I was wrong. So, needless to say, the next time the car was headed toward Ocala, Florida, I was in the driver's seat.

Now, Ocala is, was, and will always be the country. People who are into gambling on horse races know you always bet on a horse raised in Ocala. It's known as the horse capital of the world. It's hard to ride around Ocala one day and not see a truck with a trailer transporting horses attached to the back. Many of the horses from Ocala have raced in and won the Kentucky Derby. So, it was a country, but it was also huge. There are only a few buildings, no skyscrapers, and plenty of farmland.

The city of Ocala is the center of Marion County, Florida. Marion County is one of the biggest counties in the state. Marion County is bigger than some of the states in the country. It has all these little towns surrounding it, like Citra, Reddick, Zuber, and Dunnellon, but nothing was there. If you wanted to do anything in Marion County, you had to come to Ocala. So, that's where we set up shop.

Like many cities, Ocala had its own Black population. The Black people lived in Westside, Carver Park, Bugsby Quarters, Jones Side, and Happiness Homes, our main consumer base.

We found where the money was, and Ocala was a gold mind. Those country people couldn't get enough of us. We made so much money so quickly that I got scared. There was no way that we were selling out like this, and the police weren't bothering us. I made nearly one million dollars in a few months, so I made Ocala my second home.

While getting acquainted with my new surroundings, I got some people to work for me while I was out of town. I met this woman named Sherry. She was a brown-skinned woman who lived on the Westside. She didn't take any mess and said whatever came to her mind. After meeting her, I knew I needed her on my team. While negotiating the terms of the deal, she got a visitor at her home. When she opened the door, I almost fell over when I saw those shoes. I would know them anywhere. It was Chris from ACI. Turns out, he was Sherry's brother. So, I knew the deal would be set.

"So, You made it to Ocala," he said as he greeted me.

"Man, I had to come up here and see what y'all were about," I said. "Gotta make some of this money."

"I know that's right," Chris said.

"I didn't know you knew my brother," Sherry said. "I didn't even know you knew who he was," I said.

"Looks like God put us in the right place at the right time," Sherry added.

At that point in my life, I truly believed that God had set me up with someone in a strange city who I could trust to do right by me while we sold drugs. And for a while, it worked. The money started rolling in, and we were all getting paid.

My week consisted of returning to Fort Lauderdale on Monday, going to Ocala on Friday, dropping off products and picking up money, and heading to Atlanta for the weekend. By that time, my younger sister had started going to one of the colleges up there, so I decided to open an Atlanta branch of operation. I got one of her roommates to begin selling for me.

My sister knew someone who worked for a rental car company who got us a deal on renting cars. We rented new vehicles weekly to go back and forth between Atlanta and Fort Lauderdale.

I was back on top and didn't see an end in sight. Now, I could hang out again, dress like I used to, and make the moves I wanted.

There was a club in Fort Lauderdale called Big Daddies. Everyone use to be there. It would be nothing to see a Hollywood star or a big-time gangster in there on a Friday night. It was the biggest club in Fort Lauderdale, and everyone who was anyone was inside.

There would be all types of women from every walk of life, and you could pick whatever flavor you liked. One night, In December of 1978, I caught this girl out of the corner of my eye staring at me. She was brown- skinned and small. She looked like a black Barbie Doll. When I turned to look at her, she looked away like she was embarrassed. I didn't recognize her, so I knew she couldn't be from around town. I wanted to go over and talk to her, but when I looked up again, she had gotten lost in the crowd. I was gonna let it go, but something told me I would see her again.

The next weekend, right before Christmas, I saw her again. She was with her friends, and I decided to go over and talk to her.

"You should take a picture," I said as I approached. "Huh?" she said. She looked confused.

"I saw you looking at me," I said with a laugh. "You should take a picture. It'll last longer."

She smiled. "I thought I knew you." "You can know me," I said.

"Is that a good thing?" she said. "Is what a good thing?"

"To know you?"

"Oh, Baby, it's the best thing to know me. I ain't like these other niggas." "We'll see she said!"

I came to find out her name was Stephanie, and she was from Miami. She wasn't old enough to be in Big Daddies but had snuck in. She was a senior in high school, and she had so much freedom because her mother was a nurse who worked overnight. She was a pretty girl with a bright future in front of her, and I wanted to be a part of it.

Every bit of free time I got, I was spending it with Stephanie. She wondered how I got so much money to spend on her, but I told her that I had investments. She wasn't a dummy, so she just played along like she believed me. She knew I was doing things that would make her mother move her to a new state far away from me. Most of my time in Fort Lauderdale would be spent in her company, and I loved every bit.

I was on top of the world, but there is an old saying about a huge setup for a downfall, and they must've been talking about me. With all the partying and living life I was doing, I fell into a cycle that I never thought I would be in again. While at a club one night, I got introduced to a new form of cocaine called freebase. I would snort cocaine from time to time, but I was never addicted to it. It didn't run my life, but Freebase was different. I took one hit, and I was addicted. I had to have that high again, and I had to chase it.

When I got high with heroin back in the day, the high would last longer. Off of one hit, I could be high for hours, but freebase cocaine was different. It seemed like it was over as soon as the high got good. I would spend all night trying to sustain that feeling and most of the next day. Nights began to bleed into days, and those days blended into weeks. Pretty soon, getting high was all I could think about doing. When I woke up in the morning, I thought about getting high. When I finally fell asleep, I was thinking about getting high.

I started neglecting everything and everyone around me. My trips between Fort Lauderdale, Ocala, and Atlanta became less and less until they stopped altogether. I was spending more money than I could make, and I was starting to lose myself. I couldn't bear to face Stephanie, so I hid away from her. I would say I was busy or couldn't see her. I knew it was hurting her, but I couldn't let her see me down like that. I had to make a change.

Ocala would be where I would make a new start. It was already my second home, and I thought that once there, I would be able to get off drugs and back on my feet. So, I just moved to Ocala without letting anyone know. I felt horrible about walking away from Stephanie but I couldn't let her see me like I was. I would change and come back as a better man for her.

As good as my intentions were about going to Ocala, my life didn't improve. I got worser than I had ever been.

I started stealing again. Anything that wasn't nailed down, hell, even things that were nailed down, had to go with me. I was snatching purses, breaking into houses, and even stole a truck full of couches one day.

Small Fry, who had joined me in my addiction, and I were scoping out a warehouse full of home goods. Something told me to keep watch on the building because we could come up so quickly if we could get our hands on one of those delivery trucks. We wanted to get high so bad we could feel it.

A delivery truck pulled up to the road like they were getting ready to leave when the driver opened the door and hopped out. He started jogging back toward the main warehouse building. He must've left something he needed. That's when we took our chance. Fry and I jumped into the truck's cab, him in the driver seat and me in the passenger. He put the truck in drive, and it jerked hard. I could hear the couches in the back sliding against the trailer's insides.

"Nigga, what are you doing?!" I yelled. I looked around to see if the driver was coming back. He wasn't yet.

"I didn't know it was a stick!" Fry said. "I can't drive this."

"Move!" I yelled. Fry and I scrambled over each other, switching seats to get away.

We were nervous, but it looked like we could get away with it for a while. Fry and I sold most of the couches in the back and made about eight hundred dollars. One of the couches was worth that all by itself, but we just needed to get rid of them as soon as possible with as much money as possible.

We ended up going over to Sherry's house to stash the truck. We kept one of the couches back for her to pay for letting us park the truck there.

"Y'all niggas crazy!" Sherry said with a laugh as Fry and I were moving in her new stolen couch and taking out her old one. "How did y'all manage to get this truck again?"

"Well…" I began, but I was interrupted. I heard the familiar sound of a helicopter flying overhead.

Fry, Sherry, and I paused and looked at each other. Then we heard it again. A helicopter was flying over our heads, and police sirens could be heard in the distance.

"Get that fuckin' truck out of my yard and get it out now!" Sherry yelled. Fry and I were shocked and tried to think about where we could move the truck. "Move it!" Sherry yelled again. "Y'all niggas not about to have me locked up with this shit."

Fry and I ran and jumped in the truck. We could still hear the helicopters when we pulled out of Sherry's yard. The police hadn't found us yet, but they had to know it was in the area. We kept our heads on a swivel as we drove blocks away from the house.

"Where are we gon' put it?" Fry asked. "I think I know a place," I said.

There was an abandoned shopping center about four miles away from Sherry's house, and I decided to park the truck there. When we stopped the truck behind the building, we left it running. Fry and I ran faster than we probably have in our entire lives. We only stopped to catch our breaths when we thought we had put enough distance between us and the truck. We had gotten away with it, and we still had our money.

We walked to a local drug den we knew to get some freebase. I had been to this house plenty of times before when I was the one selling the drugs. I would look at the people hanging around there and almost pity them. I knew what addiction was like, but I would never be one of them. Now, I was one of them. I wonder if some of the other addicts recognized me from when I used to sell to them.

When we walked inside, there was a small television on the news, and a news lady was standing in front of the abandoned shopping center talking about the truck that had been found empty.

The news reporter said, "If you or anyone you know has any information about this crime, do not hesitate to call the police."

# Chapter 7

Getting away with stealing the truck gave me a false sense of security. I thought I was untouchable by anyone. The drugs had me so gone that I started to get sloppy with my stealing. Soon, the police were after me, and I was on the run again. I was suspected of stealing several things, and I was connected to some drug deals that were monitored by the authorities. Regularly, I would have had my head on a swivel, but the only thing I cared about was getting drugs.

I ended up getting arrested in Lake County, Florida, on robbery charges. It was almost like a relief when I entered the Lake County jail. I realized what I always knew: I could be caught and eventually would be. I didn't make it easy for them, though. I gave them a fake name so they wouldn't know my history if they did a check. But, memories of Charlie B. dying in jail because he was denied the medicine he needed to deal with his withdrawals. I didn't want to end up like him, and I wouldn't. A couple of the headaches I had to deal with from getting off freebase made me think I would join him. I made up my mind that I would die if I did not get out of jail soon.

By January of 1982, I had built up a good relationship inside the Lake County jail. I did anything and everything I could to get out of my cell. I started by handing out books to inmates who liked to read. I would use this time to scope out any unmanned exits for an escape. Then I started cutting other inmates hair. This allowed me to get into different cells and see if they were easier to break out of than mine. I wasn't that good at cutting hair, but it was good for me to form relationships with other inmates. I could have an accomplice or make them not want to tell on me when I escaped. When I was put on trash duty, I had my plan.

I would go from floor to floor and collect the trash at the end of the day, then take it to the dumpster with a fellow inmate named Jimmy. He was a tall, bright-skinned man who was nice enough. I got it in my head that one of the garbage cans we used could fit me in it.

I could ride down to the bottom and get dumped in the trash with the rest of the garbage. The guard who watched us dump the trash didn't come near the can, so I wouldn't have to worry about him peeking in and seeing me.

One day, while we were in the yard, I approached Jimmy to convince him to help me escape.

"I'm thinking about getting out of here," I said to him slyly. "Oh yeah?" Jimmy replied.

"Yeah, man. I think I'm gonna escape." I laughed a little just to see how he would react.

"I hear that, man."

"I think I'll sneak out of here in one of the garbage cans." "Okay. I'll help you."

"Huh?" I was shocked.

"I said I'll help you," Jimmy said. He looked at me like I had just asked him what the weather was that day.

"Did you hear me, nigga?" I said in a loud whisper. "I said I'm gonna get out of here."

"And I said I'll help you."

I was thrown off because he didn't take much convincing. He was down with the plan almost before I could finish saying it. We just had to execute it. So, even though I was afraid to trust him, I took a chance at escape.

One cold January day, I started to complain about not feeling well. I didn't go out to the yard when it was time, and I stayed in my cell during meal times. So, when it came time to take out the trash, the guards found someone else to take my spot on trash duty for the day. I made my bed look like I was sleeping when Jimmy came along.

"Come on, man," he whispered loudly.

I got into the bottom of the can, and he put some trash bags over me. I heard his help coming, and they both started to push the cans to the elevator that would take us to the bottom floor of the jail.

"Damn," the man said. "This thing is heavy!" "Man, shut up!" Jimmy whispered loudly.

"Is the trash always this much?" "Most days, yeah."

My stomach dropped because I knew the man would get too curious and look inside. I could hear my heart pounding as the cart rolled slowly toward the elevator.

"I don't know how y'all do this every day," the man continued complaining. "I would have been thrown out my back lifting this thing daily."

Then I heard the guard's gruff voice say, "If I knew that you would have complained this much, I would have made Hampton get out of bed and take it down."

"I'm just sayin' it's heavy," the man sighed.

"And we heard you the first time," Jimmy said. I prayed he would keep his cool with the idiot he was working with.

I calmed down slightly when I heard the elevator doors close, and we started to descend. The guard didn't check my cell, so I was almost clear. We started on the third floor, but the trash was outside next to the yard. All I needed was to be put in that dumpster, and then I would be free.

When they went to lift the garbage can, the inmate started to complain again. "It feels like a body is in here."

"Just dump it, damn!" Jimmy said.

They lifted the can and dumped me inside the dumpster. I was free, but I knew the other inmate would be too curious to walk away. So, when he peaked his head in to see what was inside, I already had my finger up to my lips and threatened him with my eyes. His eyes, however, were as big as dinner plates. His jaw hung open like he had just seen a ghost.

"What's taking y'all so long?" I heard the guard say. I could hear his footsteps getting closer.

I fixed my eyes on the inmate so he wouldn't say anything. "Nothin'," Jimmy said as he slammed the lid closed on the dumpster.

"Yeah," the other inmate added in a subdued voice. All that loud complaining from earlier was now over.

"Alright," the officer said. He didn't come any closer. "Let's get back inside." I swear my heart must've been beating louder than the FAMU marching band. I could hear it echoing while I waited inside the dumpster. I drowned out the beating long enough to hear the sound of the door shutting. They were back inside, and I was in the clear. I still waited for some time before I decided to get out.

When I felt safe, I exited the dumpster and checked my surroundings. No one was in the yard, and no one was walking by. So, I hopped out and tried to make myself look as presentable as possible.

The thing about the Lake County Jail, in those days, was that inmates were not required to wear jail uniforms. I'm sure they changed this policy after my stunt, but I got away with it for now. You could wear regular clothes, and only the guards would know you were an inmate. To people outside, you were just another person. I was wearing a white T-shirt and a pair of blue jeans. So, I would fit in fine.

I started walking down the road toward the town, but I knew this wasn't smart. Eventually, they would check to see if I was still in my cell, and they would have every police officer on the lookout for me. So, I had to think quickly. I needed someone to give me a ride to a payphone. That way, I could call Small Fry to pick me up and get out of town quickly. The city was still a couple of miles off, and I didn't want to take a chance on them, finding out I was gone before I reached it, so I devised a plan.

The people who worked in the police station's front office didn't know what I looked like. The last place they would expect an escaped convict to be was in  the front part of  the jail they had escaped from. So, I walked up to the front of the station and waited for someone to help me.

My help showed up as an old white man driving a beat-up Ford truck. I stood up as he approached and tried to sound sincere.

"Excuse me," I said. "My car broke down up the road, and I need a ride to town."

"Was it that blue Buick back down the road?' he said.

"Yes, sir," I said. "That's the one. It's been giving me hell since I bought it." "My father had a Buick when I was growing up. The damn thing was in the shop more than it was on the road." He laughed. "So, you know my pain," I said.

"Yeah. I have to go in here and handle something, but I'll give you a ride." "Thank you so much. You have no idea how much you're helping me."

My heart pounded as the older man walked to the police station. I didn't know whether he believed me or not. The broken-down Buick could have just been a story he made up so he could go inside and tell. Either way, I decided to wait.

The older man returned and gave me the ride he promised me. I couldn't believe it. God must've put that car there just for me, or so I thought. I thanked the man when he dropped me off and went to the nearest pay phone I could. Someone must've been looking out for me because I was able to find change and make a call.

"Hello," Small Fry's groggy voice said over the phone. "Fry!" I said in a loud whisper. "You gotta come get me." "Cicero?" he said. "They let you out?"

"Nah, I got out." "You escaped?"

"Yes!" I said. "I'm by an auto shop in Tavares." "Okay. I'm coming."

"Hurry up!"

I hung up with Fry and waited. I tried not to look suspicious, so I tried blending in as much as possible. Time seemed like it was ticking by so slowly as I waited. Every car was a police car, and every sound was a police officer cocking their gun and telling me to get down. When Fry finally pulled up, I dove in his backseat and lay on the floor.

"Man," he said as he pulled off. "I can't believe you did this.? "Didn't I tell you I was gonna escape?"

"Yeah."

"You know me to be a liar?" "Nah."

"Okay, now drive like you got some sense. Don't get pulled over."

Small Fry drove me to Ocala. As we drove, I could hear the sound of police sirens as we got farther away from the jail. I knew they knew I was gone.

I stayed around Ocala for a few days but knew I had to get further away. One night, a police car saw me while walking down the road. I knew they saw me because I heard him slow down and begin to back up.

I didn't wait to see if he knew who I was. I ran. I jumped over fences, ducked in backyards, and hid in bushes. I saw him ride by slowly again with his flashlight out the window. That had to be my last night.

I returned to Fort Lauderdale and stayed with my parents for a while. My mother was happy to have me home, but my father was still suspicious. He had reason to be because I didn't stop committing crimes. I was stealing and doing all sorts of things to feed my habit.

I decided to steal a Mercedes Benz and ride to Miami one day. On my way, I met this pretty young girl, and she wanted to come with me.

"Can my friends come to?" She said. "Sure," I said. "We got the room."

The girl and her three friends hopped in the car with me and we headed to Miami. They were having fun, and so was I. I was having so much fun that I didn't realize that I didn't see a stop sign, and I ran it. Then, the familiar lights of the police car were behind me.

My stomach dropped as I pulled over. I had drugs and a gun in the car, and I knew that I was headed back to jail. As the police officer approached, I took my chance. I got out and took off in a full sprint. I was running in between cars and almost caused an accident. I could hear the officer yelling at me and into his radio. He was overweight, so I wasn't worried about him catching me, but it would be a different story when his backup came.

I started running through the neighborhood and knocking on doors.

Finally, a man came to the door.

"Sir," I said. I was trying to catch my breath. "Can you hide me? I'll give you all the money I have and all my jewelry." I had a couple thousand dollars, and my jewelry was authentic and expensive. I think I almost had him, but I heard the voices of his daughters in the background.

"Don't let that man in here, Daddy," They were crying and screaming. "That's a bad man!"

The man turned back and looked at me. "I'm sorry," he said. "I can't let you in. I got my girls in here."

I didn't stay even to thank him because I had to keep running. I could hear the sound of the police cars growing louder as I continued to knock on doors and try to get someone to help me.

I eventually ended up in the courtyard of a housing project when the police caught up to me. They tackled me and jacked my arm up behind my back.

"You're gonna break my arm!" I yelled as the officers pinned me down. "You shouldn't have ran, nigger!" the officer said. He pulled my arm up higher.

By this time, people started to come out of their homes to see what was happening.

"Y'all ain't gotta do him like that," I heard the voice of an old lady say. "Don't beat him!" another woman added. "He's already on the ground." "Mind y'all business!" the officer said.

The women continued to protest my treatment, but the police didn't care. They threw me around like a rag doll till I was finally stuffed into the backseat of one of their cruisers.

They slammed me down in a chair in the interrogation room when we got to the jail.

"You know you scared those girls when you ran off like that?" The officer said. "Why'd you do it?"

I said nothing, so I sat and looked at the table. "You wanna tell us about the gun or the drugs?" I still said nothing.

"How many bodies do you have on that gun?" "Ain't no bodies on that gun," I said.

"So you can speak?" the officer said. Now that we've established that, let me get a name."

I sat quietly. I didn't want to give them my real name or the fake name I escaped under. I thought back to a childhood friend of mine and decided to use his name.

"My name is Arthur Jones," I said.

"Is that so?" The officer said. He sat down and started writing on his piece of paper. "What's your birthday, Arthur?"

I knew Arthur well from growing up. I knew his birthday, favorite color, and even his grandparent's names. I also know that Arthur had never been in trouble. The last I heard of him was that he had moved up to Tallahassee and had a good job. That comes from living in a close-knit community.

I waited in the interrogation room while the police checked Arthur's records. I didn't think he had ever been in trouble, so I wasn't worried. I was worried that they would find out I was lying about who I was and would be in more trouble.

The arresting officer returned and slammed a paper on the table. I knew that I was caught.

"Why'd you run, Arthur?" he said.

"Huh?" I said. I was so confused that I had almost forgotten that I had given him my friend's name.

"You don't even have a parking ticket. Why did you run?" "I was scared. I didn't want to get in any trouble."

"Well, now you've done it," the officer exhaled. "You're gonna be charged with possession of an illegal substance."

I tried my best to look disappointed, but I was beaming inside. I couldn't believe giving a fake name worked again. "I'm sorry."

I was booked into the Miami jail under the name Arthur Jones. Since Arthur had no previous charges, I was released to my recognizance on the day of my arraignment.

Escaping capture multiple times had done something to me. If I didn't think I was invincible before, I sure as hell knew I was then. I could do what I wanted to who I wanted, and the police would have to turn me loose if they caught me. Besides, I had the names of other childhood friends I could give them.

About one week later, I saw a man buying tires across the street from an automotive shop. He had returned to the store, so I knew this was my chance. These were brand-new tires, and I knew I could get some good money for those. So, when he was inside, I rolled the tires around to the side of the building to hide them. When he returned, he would think someone stole them and leave looking for them. Little did I know then, he saw me.

I heard the sound of a gun being cocked behind my head as I moved one of the tires. I froze.

"What are you doing with my tires?" I heard a gruff voice say. "What do you mean?" I said.

"You're trying to steal my tires!" The man's voice was growing angrier. "Nah, man," I said. "I was just moving them out of the way. I wasn't
  stealing them."

"The hell you say. You just stay right there, and we'll let the police figure this out."

"Ain't no need for that," I tried to turn around slowly, but I felt the barrel of the gun against the back of my head. "I promise I'm not stealing em."

"Don't you even think about movin'."

The man held the gun on me until the police showed up. I thought of a new name to give them for when I got to jail, but this time, they had done their due diligence. When they booked me, I was fingerprinted this time. When the officer entered the interrogation room, I knew I was had.

"Oh," he said as he looked through a stack of papers. "They are looking for you in Lake County, Mr. Hampton."

"Huh?" I said. I was confused again.

"That's who you are, isn't it?" The officer continued. "Albert Hampton?" I put my head down. Lake County had figured out who and where I was. "You're not gonna be here for long," the officer said. "We're gonna get
  somebody to drive you back where you need to be."

I was sent back to Lake County, and they welcomed me with open arms. some reason, even though I was sentenced for it, the escape charge never followed me.

No matter what court date I had or sentencing I got, my escaping from jail didn't seem to matter that much wherever I was sent to prison. My first month in prison was in high security. I knew that was because of the escape charge, but it was to a minimum security prison when I was transferred. I couldn't understand why, but I didn't question it.

While I was in prison, I was able to kick my freebase habit. I got off the drug and never went back to it, like I did with heroin. I spent most of my time in Polk County at the prison there, and while serving my time, I heard about a new drug that had the streets going wild. They were taking cocaine and cutting with baking soda. This process turned it into a rock form, and people called it crack.

"Man, I'm telling you," one of my fellow inmates said, "that shit is taking over the world. You can be a millionaire in a couple of weeks selling that shit." "Sounds like freebase to me," I said. "So, I don't know how it's different."

"I'm telling you that the money is different. Crack is the future."

I kept this information in my head until I got out, whenever that was. I was stuck in prison for the next ten years, and I didn't know how I was going to make it. All my other bids had been only a couple of years at the most, but a whole decade was something different.

Someone else I knew was also in prison, and he was sentenced to a similar time as me. He was supposed to make a ten-year bid but was about to get out when he had only served six years. He told me that there was this new thing called contract parole. You could write the parole board and make them a promise what you would do in a certain amount of time if you were released from prison. This could be getting your GED, enrolling in college, getting a job, paying restitution to victims, etc. It could be anything, and you would have to make progress on those things, or you risk violating your parole and being sent back to prison to serve the rest of your time.

Well, as soon as he told me about it, I wrote the parole board to try to get out. I told them I would enroll in college courses and get a job to repay the community for what I had done. I waited weeks for news to come, and I got the best present right before Christmas. I was going to be released.

I got out of prison, and I vowed never to go back. I wasn't going to let drugs ruin my life. I wouldn't even experiment with anything hard again, and I would keep my head straight. That thought worked for a while.

# Chapter 8

There's a saying that has been around forever. "The lion is the king of the jungle." Now, if we look at the statistics of nature, we will find that the lion is not the fastest, most intelligent, or strongest; hell, the lion is not even in the jungle. But still, people call him the king. That is for one reason, he believes he is the king. The lion struts around and acts like he knows what is and isn't, and all the other animals treat him as such. I decided that this time around, I would be the lion. I would become the king of the jungle, the streets. I would be the one to set the standard for everyone around me.

When I arrived in Fort Lauderdale in December 1985, I planned to make the most money I had ever had. So, I worked to make that my reality for the next six months. It turns out the man I met in prison was right; the new drug called "Crack" was taking over the world in a big way, and the people who were selling it were making too much money to count. I had to be a part of it. Crack was doing something I had never seen before.

I had sold everything under the sun, but nothing could compare to the way people were hooked on crack. I couldn't remember if I was ever as stung out as these new "crackheads" that roamed the streets. They looked like something out of a horror movie. They were willing to do anything and everything for their next fix. I met a nice-looking girl that December, but she was no longer pretty by the time April rolled around. She had gotten hooked on crack, and she was turning tricks to feed her addiction. She was just one of many. Crack could turn the most upstanding citizen into a zombie.

I couldn't think about what crack was doing to people back then. All I could think about was regaining what I had lost and never putting myself in the position to lose it again. So, I started selling crack like there was no tomorrow. I made good money while in Fort Lauderdale, but I knew the money would be made in Ocala.

In June of 1986, I went back to Ocala to start selling drugs. As I suspected, all my money would come from Ocala. I couldn't keep the crack on me.

The first night I was there, I sold out of my supply and had people beating on my door for more.

Between June and July 1986, I made seventy thousand dollars. The business was so good that I couldn't do it alone. I enlisted the help of my best friend, Small Fry, my little sister, and my father. I couldn't believe he would help me do something like this, but I appreciated the help. He and my mother were getting older, and they needed help. So, he decided to join me in making money.

On one July day, we were all in Ocala on business. We had rented a car and came up to sell some crack. I went out by myself to run some errands and left my father, my sister, and my sister's boyfriend at the hotel where we were staying. For some reason, the police got behind me. I had a lot of drugs in the car, and I knew that if I got pulled over, I was going back to jail. When they pulled me over, I did the only thing I could do. I ran. I left everything in the car except my ID, and I ran. The police chased me for a while, but couldn't catch me.

Once I escaped from the police, I found a phone booth. I called my father back at the hotel and told him to call the car rental company since it was in his name. I told him to tell them the police got the car and its location. I also told him not to call from the hotel. They could redial the number and figure out where he was. After repeating this fact repeatedly, he said he had it and would call the car rental company.

Growing up, the only problem my father had with drugs was drinking. Seeing him drunk made me never want to be drunk in my life. Now, he was trying something different. My father waited till he was in his sixties to take hard drugs. He had taken to putting cocaine in his marijuana joint and smoking it. Some people call it "Geekin," and some call it "Boonkin," but I couldn't figure out why my father decided to try it in his sixties.

So, instead of doing as I said and calling from a payphone away from the hotel, my father was high on drugs and called directly from the hotel room. When the car rental place dialed the number back, they got to the front desk and knew precisely where he was.

The police showed up at the room's door and came in. They found drugs, guns, scales, and all the paraphernalia that we were using. My father and Small Fry were arrested on the spot. My sister and her boyfriend were in the room next door, so the police did not know to check their room.

When I returned to the hotel, I went to see my sister. She and her boyfriend were in the room, and I was glad because that's where we kept the money. When I asked for it, fifteen thousand dollars was missing.

"Where's the rest?" I asked my sister. "That's all of it," she said.

"Hell no!" I shouted. "I got money missing."

"I don't know what you're talking about," my sister said. "I'm saying y'all niggas got my money."

"Nah, man," her boyfriend chimed in. "We didn't take anything."

I looked at my sister's boyfriend. I didn't think about how I didn't notice it then, but he had an addiction. He was hooked on something, which was just made clear to me. He was twitching and scratching, and his energy was just erratic.

"Maybe the police got it," he said again.

"How, mothafucka?" I roared. "The police didn't bust y'all room!"

"Oh," my sister said, "the maid did come in this morning. She must've got it."

"Now it's the maid?" I said. "Who else you got in your rolodex? Was it Colonel Mustard in the library with the candle stick?"

"Man, go on somewhere with all of that," my sister said. "I'm telling you, we don't have it!"

"Now!" I said. "You don't have it now because this nigga done put it up his nose or in a pipe."

"Come on, man," my sister's boyfriend said. I wouldn't do that to you."

"Nigga, if you weren't here with my sister, I'd put a bullet right between your eyes."

"Please!" my sister said. She jumped up to get in between me and her boyfriend. I hadn't realized it, but I had my hand on my gun. "The maid did come in today. She has to be the one who's got it. We wouldn't do that to you, Albert!"

Between Daddy and Fry being locked up and my money being gone, I was liable to do anything at that point.

My father ended up getting probation for his part in the drugs. Since he didn't have a record, they went easy on him. Small Fry, on the other hand, didn't get off so easily. He ended up doing ten months of a sentence of one year and a day.

Even though I was still mad at my sister and her boyfriend, I decided to get back to work. I focused on completing my commitments with my parole and making as much money as possible. More than ever, my connections in Ocala flourished, and I made a considerable investment.

There was a hustler who was a well-respected man in Ocala. He had his own game he was running in town, and I thought it only made sense for us to join forces. There was no need to fight over territory when there was enough money for everyone. So, one day, I went to his house to meet with him to discuss business when I saw something or someone who caught my eye.

This young woman, who was as pretty as she wanted to be, was wearing a yellow dress. I was so taken aback that I almost forgot what I came for. I wanted to get to know her and find out what she was doing hanging around there.

"Your eyes gon' pop out your head!" he said. He slapped me on my shoulder and started laughing.

"Renee!" He called the woman. "Come here." She walked over and looked at me shyly. I tried to appear as calm as possible, but I was also nervous. "This is Cicero," he said. "We're doing some business together." Renee reached out her hand, and I shook it.

"How are you doing?" I said. I think my voice may have cracked a little. "I'm doing good," Renee responded.

She walked away, and her father and I worked out a deal to make us a lot of money.

That wasn't the last I saw of Renee, though. I started hanging around her father's house more often; before you know it, we were a thing. We were going places doing things, and I was in an adult relationship for the first time in my life. Other than Stephanie, I wasn't settled enough to be in a relationship long enough for anyone to matter, but now I was.

One day, Renee came to me and told me that she was pregnant and I would be a father for the first time. I was so overwhelmed that I didn't know what to do. I never gave much thought to children, but now that I knew one was on the way, I would have to work extra hard to make sure that the troubles of my life didn't affect him.

As the months went on in her pregnancy, Renee and I started bumping heads. I felt like two people were in our relationship, but she felt like there was room for a third, her mother. I felt like her mother was too involved in what we were doing as a couple and soon-to-be parents, and I felt like her mother had her ear more than I did. So, I knew that our relationship was not going to last. And before my son arrived, our relationship was over.

The first time I held Champ in the hospital, I felt like God had given me a new lease on life. I had someone other than myself to think about in this world, and I was hell bent on making things better for him.

I decided to expand my operation to Chicago. This was tricky because I was still on probation. So, I had to ensure I was in Florida to check in with my parole officer and run my business out of the state. An old friend of mine,

Lump, from back in the day, had made a new home in Chicago. Even though we didn't meet on the best of terms, we became excellent friends, and I trusted him. He would look over things while I was in Florida handling things.

I would fly in from Chicago, see my parole officer, see Champ, and then I was back on the plane to Chicago. This was my routine for the next couple of years. I managed to run my businesses and stay out of trouble for a long while. During the 80s, Crack had run rampant through America, and people were tired of it. They were calling it an epidemic, and the people who were selling the drug were getting locked up for a long time. The politicians kept upping the amount of time someone would spend in jail for selling Crack; They put mandatory minimum sentencing in place, saying that one hundred to one crack was worse than cocaine. Selling five grams of crack would get you locked up for five years without question. By that time contracted parolewas over, and you would do every bit of that sentence.

The police were starting to get tough on crime, too. A decade prior, I was scared I made so much money in Ocala, but now I had reason to be. I saw people who I used to run the streets with getting locked up for decades. I knew I had to do something different because the streets were getting too hot. I did what all the intelligent gangsters did: I used my drug money to open a legitimate business. I opened any business I could make some money off of. I opened a photo studio, a restaurant, and a trucking business. The trucking business brought me the most money.

Businesses paid good money to have their goods hauled across America. I even made enough money to hire some guys to work for me, and they made good money. Pretty soon, I didn't have to keep selling drugs because all of my legitimate businesses were making enough money to sustain my lifestyle.

I found love for the pool game again. Even though I didn't play like I used to, I was still the baddest man to hold a cue. I wasn't playing competitively but I forgot how the game made me feel. I would play a game and consider how far I had come since being a thirteen-year-old on 27th Ave. I had done well and escaped a life that led to anyone who decided to live it.

I even managed to find love again. In 1987, I met my first wife in a club in Gainesville, FL, called the Village Traffic. We fell in love and had Chris and Shakira within the next three years. We built a house from the ground up and made a home for our family. I was now a husband and father of three, and I loved it. Nothing could come between me and my kids. I had built a great life for them.

One night in 1992, my wife, Sabrina, worked on her degree at night school. I had Shakira and Chris with me, and I planned to cook dinner for us and get them ready for bed. I pulled up to the back door of our home and got the kids situated. I took them inside and returned to get the fish I planned on cooking.

I couldn't put my finger on it then, but I felt something was wrong. The air didn't even feel the same that night. I tried to shake it off, but the feeling wouldn't disappear. I had the fish in my hand and started back inside the house when I heard one of the bushes move. I probably would have thought it was a squirrel or a bird, but then I felt something against my back.

"If you turn around, I'll blow yo fuckin' head off, nigga!" a gruff voice said from behind me. I could feel the barrel of the gun pressed against my back.

"Man, my kids are in the house," I pleaded. "Please don't do this."

"Shut the fuck up!" he said again. A man dressed in all black pushed past me and entered the house. My heart dropped when I knew he would be near my kids.

"Don't hurt my children!" I yelled. "You can have anything! Just don't hurt them."

"Take me to the safe!" the man with the gun said from behind me.

I could already hear my children starting to scream when the man found them. I couldn't think of anything else but the ways I was going to kill these two men who had come into my home and terrorized my children.

"Take me to the fuckin' safe, or I'mma kill them kids!" The man yelled again.

"Safe," I thought to myself. "How does this nigga know I have a safe?" I had a safe, but it was empty, and only people I knew personally knew about it. The man started walking me toward the direction of my shed where the safe was, so I knew somebody in my circle was in on the take, and they were playing with my children's lives.

As we walked toward the shed, I was shaking so badly that I tripped over my shoes and stumbled.

"Please, man!" I kept repeating. "You can have anything. Just don't hurt my babies!"

"Shut up, nigga!" he yelled. "If you don't give me this money, they gon' have a big funeral for you and all the children next weekend." My stomach dropped when he said this.

"Please.."

"Shut the fuck up, and don't look at me!"

I could hear my kids screaming at the top of their lungs. I could only imagine the things that man was doing to them. I made up my mind that day I was going to kill both of them and make sure it was a slow and painful death. They would pay for this.

I didn't even remember where the safe was when we finally reached the shed. I couldn't find the light switch, and my words were jumbled.

"Where's the safe!?" the man yelled. All I could hear was my babies screaming, and all I could think about was killing these men.

We found the safe sitting in the corner on a counter. He led me over to it, and I stumbled over the numbers. Was the code my birthday? No, it was Champ's birthday. No, Sabrina's. No, my mama's. Or was it the area code for Fort Lauderdale? I could barely think straight.

"Nigga, you got ten seconds!"

I finally put in the code, and the door swung open. The man with the gun to my back found out what I already knew. There was no money. I had gone legit, and like all legit businessmen, my money was locked away in a bank, not a shed.

The man cocked the gun and put it to the back of my head. "Where's the money?"

My entire body started to shake. I didn't care if he killed me. I didn't want anything to happen to my babies. I didn't want Sabrina to come home and find the children dead in the house.

"I don't have a lot of money on me. It's in the bank." I said. "You want your kids to die?" he said.

"It's true!" I said, pleading. "All I got is a couple hundred in my wallet. You can have that and whatever you want out of the house, but don't hurt my babies."

The man reached into my pocket and fumbled around for my wallet. He found it and took the money in it.

"What else you got?" the man said.

"I got this jewelry!" I said. I put my hands up to showcase the real gold rings I had on my hands and the gold necklace around my neck. He started removing the rings and putting them in his pocket. "You can have anything else you want out of the house too: TVs, furniture, food. Just don't hurt my kids, man."

"Shut up!"

I felt the barrel of the gun leave my back, and I was about to breathe a sigh of relief. Then I felt the worst pain I had ever felt in my life. I dropped down to my knees as I was shot five more times. As I lay bleeding out on the floor of the shed, I could hear my babies crying in the distance.

# Chapter 9

I came to in the hospital, and the first thing I could do was yell. "Chris! Shakira!"

"They're alright!" Sabrina said. She was sitting on the side of my bed.

I looked around the room and tried to gather my thoughts. The only thing I could think of was how I was going to kill those men. Then I felt a hand on mine. My mother sat on the other side of the bed. I could tell that she had been crying, and she looked tired.

"I'm sorry, Mama," I said, holding back tears.

"It's okay, baby," she said. She stroked my cheek. "God has you." She began to cry.

"What happened?" Sabrina said.

I told Sabrina and my mother what happened at the house that night. Someone in the neighborhood heard the shots and called the police. They found the children in the house unharmed, but they found me in the shed, on the floor, and bleeding out.

I was shot six times in the back and leg. I required major surgery to correct the problems caused by the bullets. It was almost six months before I could walk again, but the pins that were placed in my leg remain to this day. During the recovery, and every day after, all I could do was think about who did this to me and who in my circle had snitched about the safe. Over the years, I ensured that I kept my circle tight. I had seen too many tales of hustlers who became big-time only to be done in by someone in their circle. There would always be too many people to keep track of. An informant, a mole, or a rival could easily infiltrate their ranks and bring the whole operation down. At the height of my game, I only had eight people working under me. These people were loyal, and I could trust them, so I didn't know who to suspect.

For months after the incident, they haunted me. I would go to sleep and dream of the day I would kill the men who did this to me. I would sometimes wake up in the middle of the night and leave the house. I would stay out all night, driving around and asking anyone if they knew anything about what happened and who could have done it. I offered a bounty to anyone with information about who did it. I was visiting all of the trap houses that had been in my rear view for some time to ask for information.

I kept my ear to the streets to see who knew what until I finally got a tip. A friend of mine was out when they heard someone bragging about a robbery they committed and how they left the man on the floor bleeding.

"I got some information for you, Ro, " my friend said to me.

"What ya got?" I said. My stomach tensed in anticipation for news I had been waiting for months to hear.

"I know who did it." "Who?!"

"Two niggas named Marcus and Emmett. They heard you had some money and were gonna rob you. Somebody told them about the safe in your garage, and how that's where you kept all the money."

"Who told them that?"

"I don't know man, but I know it was them who did it because they described the inside of your house.:"

"Thank you," was all I could say.

I now had my names, but I didn't know my mole. Who was talking about my house and what I had in there? On that front, all I could do was close ranks. If you weren't close to me, then you wouldn't be around me. No one could come to my house unless you knew me personally. Friends and acquaintances were forbidden. On the other front, I had my suspects, and now it was time to catch them.

Marcus Harvey was a low-level street dude. He and his friend Emmett Knowles were nothing more than wannabe gangsters who would never amount to much. They made stupid mistakes in their lives of crime, selling drugs to undercover police officers, robbing people they knew, and getting cheated out of money. The dumbest mistake they made, however, was when they decided they were going to rob me and hold my children hostage.

I was on the hunt. I knew who to look for when leaving the house at night. Anywhere they were expected to be, I was there. I would keep my hand on my hip and fantasize about seeing them in a crowd and unleashing all my fury on them.

I thought about sitting outside their parents' houses, or better yet, I would take their parents hostage and show them what it feels like. Maybe if I were to put a bullet in one of their mamas, they would know how it feels to be helpless when someone you love screams for their life.

What I didn't recognize then, but I recognize now, is that what I was doing was making the people around me feel unsafe. The nights I spent running around in the streets looking for the people who attacked my family, I was neglecting them. I left my wife and kids alone in the same house that we were attacked in. They could have come back in the middle of the night and killed my family to show me a lesson for pursuing them, but I didn't care. I had to prove something to them and to everyone.

I thought about putting a hit out on them. I had money, and people would do anything for some cash, but I wanted this revenge to be personal. I couldn't just hear about them being killed, I had to be the one to pull the trigger. I needed to see life leave their eyes so I could sleep at night, so my family would be safe again.

On one of my nightly prowls, I saw Marcus. I knew it had to be him. He looked exactly like he was described to me. He was a skinny, nappy-headed boy. He was probably walking around looking for some house to rob or meet some unlucky man to rob, but he saw me, and now his night was unlucky. He knew it too. I may as well have been the ghost of Christomas future because all the life drained out of his face when our eyes met.

I didn't have time to react because he took off. He had run and was now hiding somewhere. That didn't stop me. I kept looking for him all night. I was walking between houses, checking in people's backyards, and acting like I was a police officer myself. I kept looking for him until the sun rose, and it seemed like he had vanished. It had been months since the shooting, and it seemed like I was never going to find him, so I turned to an unlikely resource to catch him.

I walked into the Ocala police department and gave them the names of the people who shot me and held my children captive. I never thought that I would be the person to go to the police about anything, but I needed them to find the both of them. I didn't want to bring them to legal justice; I still wanted street justice. I wanted to be on the scene when the police arrested them so I could walk up to the squad car while they were sitting in the back, open the door, shoot them, and then be on my way. Or maybe I could commit a crime to end up in jail with them. That way, I would be able to strangle them to death or beat them with something.

All I lost physically was a couple of rings and five hundred dollars. The scars on my legs healed, but they took something else from me. They made me feel unsafe in my own home. I wasn't able to sleep well at night, knowing that they were walking around like nothing had happened or that they thought it was okay to do that to my family. Revenge had to be had. Not just for them, but also to show anyone else who thought they could come to Albert "Cicero" Hampton's house and mess with his family.

When the police finally caught my attacker, it was a bittersweet moment. I needed to know where he was, but I was upset that the police found him before I did. They may have put some extra effort into the mission. I told them it would be better if they saw them first because I wouldn't stop looking. And if I ran across them, there would be no witnesses to tell them what happened.

My attacker was charged with three counts of false imprisonment, one count of robbery, one count of attempted murder, and two counts of kidnapping a minor. I wish I could put a bullet in him for every charge he had. Of course, he pleaded not guilty and refused to give up the partner he was with in the house. But I knew who he was. If I could make it through the trial, the state could have Marcus, and I would take care of Emmett. Now, I had to sit in court and testify against the man who tried to kill my family.

"Mr. Hampton?" The defense attorney said to me. "Mr. Hampton, did you understand the question?"

I stared at Marcus Harvey like a wolf on the hunt during the trial. I had worked it out in my head how I would get the gun away from the bailiff and shoot him dead. Maybe I could take the bailiff's nightstick and beat him to death. Or I could take one of the flag poles behind the judge and ram it through his chest. I would stand there satisfied as his mother watched her child bleed to death on the courtroom floor. I could also…

"Mr Hampton?" The defense attorney called me again. "Yes?" I said.

"So, you did see my client's face on the night you were shot?" he said. "No," I said. "Well, kinda. I couldn't get a good look at him because it was dark, and he wouldn't let me turn around all the way."

"So, you can't say with one hundred percent certainty that it was my client who shot you in the back?"

"Yes, I can."

"How, Mr. Hampton? You just told the court that you couldn't get a good look at him. The person who shot you told you not to turn around."

"I heard his voice," I said.

"Do you know what voice actors are, Mr. Hampton?" "Objection," the prosecutor said. "Relevance?"

"I promise I'm going somewhere with this, your honor," the defense attorney said.

"Get there quick, counselor," the judge said. "Overruled."

"Do you know what voice actors are, Mr. Hampton?" the defense attorney continued.

"Yes," I said. I was getting aggravated, but I tried not to show it. I was liable to snap and beat the hell out of him for his client. I found Sabrina's face in the courtroom, and she looked at me reassuredly. This helped keep me calm during the trial.

"So, you know that people can constantly change their voices?" the attorney continued.

"Yes," I said.

"Then, is it possible that the person who shot you in the back could have been changing their voice to sound like my client?"

"Objection, your honor," the prosecution interrupted again. "Speculation." "Sustained," the judge said.

"Let me rephrase that," the defense attorney said. "You do know that people can change their voices, correct?"

"Yes," I said.

"So, is it possible that the person who shot you in the back was changing their voice?"

"I guess. I don't know."

"Mr. Hampton," the attorney had switched to some fake contrite voice that made my skin crawl. "I know that you and your family have gone through something traumatic. I wouldn't wish this on my worst enemy. I also believe the person who did this to you should be brought to justice, but you can not say beyond a reasonable doubt that the person was or is my client."

"It was him," I said.

"There is no way you could know that for…"

"I know it was him! I can tell by his smile that it was him!" "Mr. Hampton, sit down," the judge banged his gavel. "You think this shit funny, nigga?!" I yelled.

"Mr. Hampton, sit down, or you will be held in contempt!" the judge banged his gavel again.

"I have no further questions, your honor," the defense lawyer said as he sat behind the desk.

When I got off the stand, I knew that he had gotten away with it. I, of all people, knew better than to trust the police to do right by me. In their eyes, we were just some niggers doing what niggers do. If I would have died, or if my children would have died, they would have put no more effort into getting justice for us. We would just be more names to add to the statistics about niggers killing each other.

So, I spent the majority of the deliberation trying to think of ways to kill him when I saw him on the street. He would pay for this one way or the other and he would wish that it was the police who caught up to him instead of me.

The jury found Marcus Harvey not guilty on all charges because I could not positively identify him, they couldn't convict him on the word of a friend of mine. The prosecutor approached me after the trial, saying he was sorry that it worked out this way, but I didn't care if he went to jail. I didn't want him to go to jail. I still wanted to kill him myself. All I was using the court for was to get him, so I could stop searching for him all night.

The court system may have let him go, but I wouldn't. I would catch up to him and make him pay.

# Chapter 10

After losing in court, I became paranoid. I still wanted to find Marcus and Emmett to make them pay for what they did to me. Since I didn't know who had told them about the safe, I couldn't trust people around my home. Everyone was a suspect, and everyone was plotting on me in some way. I checked my surroundings when I would get out of the car at home, especially at night. I would have my hand on my gun and my finger on the trigger. I would throw rocks at the bushes to see if anyone was there. A couple of squirrels almost caught bullets a few times.

I didn't stop looking for my attackers. I would still get up in the middle of the night to find them. Marcus said he couldn't have been the one who shot me because he was at a friend's house that night. So, I stalked that friend's house, looking for him. I knew all his hangout spots and all his buddies. They knew I was looking for him and wanted him to know I was looking for him. I wanted him to never feel safe. I wanted him to sleep with one eye open until I could close both of them permanently for him.

I ran into the friend who said he was at his house the night I was shot one day at the store.

"Your friend has been to your house lately?" I asked. I looked him dead in his eye to intimidate him.

"Look man," he said. His voice trembled. "I ain't got nothing to do with that."

"Really?" I said. "You sat up there on that stand and lied when you knew that nigga wasn't at your house."

"He was there that day."

"Don't play word games with me, nigga!" I put my hand on my hip where I kept my gun holstered. I was liable to shoot him right there just for playing with me. "He might have been there that day, but that night that nigga and his friend had my children in the house screamin'!"

"Aye," he said. He looked down at my hip and started to back up slowly. "I just said what I saw. I wasn't there."

"Don't be there when I catch ya friends either." I said. I backed away and took my hand off my hip.

Marcus and Emmett made themselves scarce around Ocala. I couldn't find them anywhere. I even started checking in Gainesville and Orlando to see if they were hiding out there. They knew since the law didn't catch them, it would only be a matter of time before I would. My head stayed on a swivel looking for those punks, and nothing, not even my family could stop me from getting my payback.

What made it worse was that people on the street started to think that because I never caught them, they could try me too. I heard whispers of me getting soft, and I knew it would be a matter of time before some young dummy would get it in his mind to do something stupid to me.

So, I wasn't surprised when I got word one night that one of my truck drivers got robbed, and my truck had been shot up. The driver was ok, but the truck would require thousands of dollars in repairs. Now, I knew people were messing with me. They saw how the boys who held me hostage got off, and now they thought it was open season. I couldn't let this trespass go unpunished.

The boy who shot at my truck was named Darius Johnson. He was some seventeen-year-old troublemaker who caused nothing but problems for everyone he came in contact with. I might have identified with him because of my troubled youth, but he took things to a level that I never thought of taking them. He was known to jump on his mother on any occasion. I fought with my classmates and friends, but he fought with everyone. He once stood outside of someone's house and yelled at them that he was going to rob them. People hated seeing him coming, and he thought shooting at one of my trucks was a good idea.

One night, Fry and I sat at an Ocala gas station. Everyone calls it the "Big Midget." I had heard that Darius would rob me next. So, I was going to be prepared no matter what happened. I wouldn't run or be scared because it was all people would think you would do once you got that reputation.

As Fry and I sat in front of the store, I noticed the same car drive back and forth several times. It doesn't take a rocket scientist to know they were scoping the scene to figure out who they could rob.

"Hey, man," I said to Fry. "I think you should go." "Nah," Fry said, "I'm good."

oldest friends, so he could tell when my mind was working. "You sure?

Because I ain't got nowhere to be."

"I told you I'm good," I said. "I'll catch up with you later."

Fry reluctantly agreed. "Alright, man," he sighed. "Holla at me later." I told Fry goodbye and sat in my car.

The car that was driving back and forth then pulled into the parking lot. They didn't pull into a space but parked parallel to the road. I could see someone get out of the car in my rearview mirror. I had my hand on my gun, and I put it like I was ready to shoot as soon as someone got close enough to the car. As the man approached, I rolled down my window. I could see it was Darius.

He saw the gun poked out of the window and stopped. As he turned to run, he said, "Man, that wasn't me!"

I started shooting at him as he ran. I didn't count how many bullets hit him, but all I knew was I couldn't find him. I looked between cars and checked behind the building, but he was gone. I thought I missed all my shots because I couldn't find him anywhere.

The police were on the scene a few minutes after the shots because the Big Midget was only a few blocks from the police station. They questioned me about what happened, and I gave them the story. After some time, word came back that Darius had made it to the hospital, which was also in the area, but he had succumbed to his wounds and died. I was now under arrest for second-degree murder.

The judge granted me a bond, and I was out until trial. I hired a lawyer and prepared my case. I was told it was going to be an uphill battle because the boy was running away from me when I shot him. Even though I told him the other circumstances, he wasn't a threat to me then. One crazy thought that kept playing in my mind was ,"At least everyone knew that I wasn't to be played with." That thought made me feel safer for a time. Even though I was looking at decades behind bars, I had a strange sense of peace knowing that I had earned back whatever respect I had lost for not getting the people who robbed me and held my children hostage.

Of course, Darius's family wasn't happy about his death. I understood them, though. Even if one of mine turned out to be the worst human being ever to walk the earth, I would still love them and want them to be here with me. Parents aren't supposed to bury their children, but I had made Darius's mother bury him.  She wanted justice for her son and tried to make it seem like he was some good boy who was killed by a monster when the truth probably was he might have beaten her to death one day if my bullet hadn't stopped him that night.

I didn't hold it against anyone who loved him, though. I was just in a situation where I could have lost my children, and I still wanted them dead. I didn't feel that bad about it. I knew he was going to try to take my life or rob me if he had the chance. It was either me or him, and I had to choose that it would be him.

Even though my involvement with the drug game had cooled down during this time, I still kept it going some just to keep my options open. It probably wasn't the smartest thing to do while out on bond, but I decided to chance it. It was now going on two years, and I still hadn't been to trial on my murder case. The state needed time to gather evidence, and they were having a hard time trying to paint Darius as a harmless victim, given his history in the community.

One weekend, I was headed back to Ocala from Fort Lauderdale. I had picked up some weed, and I was going to take it back to sell it in Ocala. During this "tough on crime" time, police became extra observant of cars leaving the south of Florida and heading north, especially if Black men drove them. So, when the police car got behind me, I became a little nervous, but I wasn't worried. I always followed the laws of the road, and none of my lights were out on my car. That was my main rule for traveling, and I never forgot it. The only thing is the police officer stayed behind me for the longest time. When I switched lanes, he changed lanes. When I would brake, he would brake. At this point, there was no doubt that I was being followed, and it would be a matter of time before he found some reason to pull me over. Going to jail for the possession of marijuana wouldn't look good while I was out on bond for second-degree murder. So, I decided to play it cool.

I pulled into a rest station on the side of the highway. The officer kept going, so I thought I was in the clear. I stayed around at the rest area for a while to make sure. But when I pulled back out on the road, the police officer was behind me again. He followed me down the road for another ten miles. I repeatedly looked down at the needle on the speedometer, checked my lanes, and watched the officer in the rearview. He followed behind until I pulled into a gas station.

This time, the officer exited his car at the pump and started walking toward my car. I waited until he got to my bumper, and I peeled out of the parking lot like a bat out of hell. The officer was left scrambling and running back to his car.

I didn't see him behind me, so I started throwing the drugs out the window as quickly as I could. I knew that I would be caught, but adding drugs to a murder charge would put me away for life.

When I pulled over, the police ordered me out of the car with his weapon drawn. I complied and was placed under arrest. My days of playing football must've paid off because they could not find those drugs anywhere.

"I'm still arresting you," the officer said.

"For what?" I responded. "I didn't even have anything on me."

"You didn't stop when I put on my lights," he responded. "Under Florida law, that's called Battery on a Law Enforcement Officer." It was a new law that had just been put in the books. Because I took the officer on a high-speed chase, it put my life, his life, and other people's lives in potential danger. It could carry up to fifteen years of jail time if I were convicted.

Now, the attorneys in my murder trial were ready to go to trial. They had proof that I couldn't behave while out on bond. The jury would hear battery on LEO and think that I had been in a fight with the police. Combined with the murder charge, there wouldn't be a jury in the world who wouldn't see me as a violent criminal who needed to be locked away from society.

The state appointed me a paid lawyer for my case. Even though he was a good attorney, he didn't really want to work on my case. He came in the door telling me I should plead guilty and accept whatever the state was offering.

"They want to give you five years on the murder charge and fifteen for the battery on a LEO," my attorney said.

"Twenty years?" I questioned. I didn't know if I was more shocked at the number of years or the fact that the murder charge was carrying less time than the battery charge. "I'm not doing twenty years."

"We could take it to court, and you could get life," he responded. "You are a habitual offender with a history of violent crime. I do not suggest we take this to trial."

"You can't do any better than twenty years?" I had been to prison three times already, so I was well acquainted with the system. I knew there was always a deal to be made. "Tell them I'll take twenty years with eight suspended." I knew my time would be reduced by a third when I got to Lake Butler, and I would be out in eight years. My attorney returned the deal to the prosecution, and they agreed to the terms.

I ended up in a prison in a town called Coleman in Sumter County, FL. When I arrived at the prison, one of the guards approached me and asked me if I knew Marcus Harvey.

"Yes," I said. "I know him." I tried to conceal my feelings toward my attacker from the guard.

"Well," he said, "he's here in the prison, and he's taken out an order of separation on you."

That's why I couldn't find him. He was in prison on an unrelated charge, and I thought he must've run out of the state of Florida.

"What does that mean?" I said.

"It's like he has a restraining order on you while you two are in the same camp," he said. "We'll keep you two separated at all times so we don't have any problems."

"I won't cause any problems to that man," I lied. I needed to get as close to him as I could.

"He says that you have a vendetta against him and would take revenge if you got the chance," the guard said. He was reading off a paper that held the complaint.

"That's all in the past. I promise."

The guard looked at me and sighed. "Just to be sure, we'll keep you two separated. He won't even be on this side of the camp."

My heart sank. I was as close as possible, and he was still out of reach. I lay in my bed at night and thought about how I would sneak over to the other side of the camp and kill him in his bunk. I had escaped from jail once. It couldn't be that hard to escape from my cell and reach the other side of the prison. I would lay in my bunk at night thinking about how to get over to Marcus, but the opportunity would never come. I didn't lay eyes on him the entire time we were in prison. All four years and eleven months that I spent in prison, I spent knowing he was just a few hundred yards away.

# Chapter 11

In 1999, I was released from prison. Being locked up for almost five years was not good for business. I had to get back on my feet and provide for my family. The best way I knew to do that was to return to the streets. I spent the holidays with my family, but at the beginning of the year, I had an empire to rebuild.

By the year 2000, crack was out of style. People still smoked it, but after the havoc that it wreaked on communities around America and the tough-on-crime policies made by politicians, the customer base had dried up considerably. So, I went back to what I knew. I was selling cocaine and marijuana. I started hanging around Miami more to build up my connections. The people in Ocala still didn't have access to quality drugs without me.

One of my best connections was this Colombian woman they call the "Cocaine Godmother." Griselda Blanco was a short, round woman who looked like she should have been baking cookies for her kids, but she was one of the deadliest gangsters in Miami. Everyone knew not to play with her or her money. When I met her, you could have sworn that we had stepped on the set of "Scarface." I half expected for Al Pacino to walk out of the back room at any moment. Everyone around Griselda respected and feared her. She barely had to speak and people would move like they knew what she was going to say.

I kept my cool, though. I talked to her nicely and made her laugh. Just like most people in my life, I had charmed the Cocaine Godmother. That night, she gave me 13 kilos of cocaine and wouldn't accept any payment for it.

"No, just bring me the money back when you sell all this," she said. It was the first time since Charlie B that someone didn't ask me for the money upfront for the drugs I was selling.

Griselda would get busted by the feds a few months after our meeting. Everyone felt she was still out because she was trying to get information to turn others in. So, I distanced myself from her. My sister told me she would come looking for me. I would be out of town or out of state, and I would tell my sister to make up some lie about where I was. I smelled a rat and didn't want any parts of it.

The last time I let my small circle get a little too big, I ended up with bullets in my legs. I couldn't risk being involved with anyone who was even being thought of by the feds.

I was able to get back into the trucking business from the money I made from selling drugs. I got a few trucks, and it was business as usual. I was able to get my family back to the life they had become accustomed to, and it was like the early 90s again. I bought houses and cars and was living life, but time takes a toll on us all.

While I was in prison, my father was diagnosed with throat cancer in 1998. The doctors gave him six months to live, but they didn't know what I knew. I knew my father was a fighter. I knew it wouldn't be easy to take him out like that. Cancer would be a walk in the park if he could raise me and put up with all the foolishness I put him through. My father beat those six months and then some. He lasted five years on a six-month diagnosis. On August 6, 2003, my father lay down on one side and woke up on the other.

As I looked over my father in his casket, I thought about all the memories that we had together. Most of them involved me getting whooped for something I did, but they were our memories. I thought about how much of a handful I was and how I must've kept him and Mama up at night while I ran the streets. Now, he could sleep and not worry about any of the crazy things I was doing.

Over the years, I had become a legend around the Ocala area. Some of the younger men in the area started to look up to me and held me in high regard. People like the future NFL star Daunte Culpepper would become permanent fixtures in my life. He and his friends like Larry Tucker and Kenny Clark would look out for me and have me around to tell them the crazy stories about my life. They also wanted to try to play with me in a game of pool. I never let any of those jokers win. I would be in all places with them and wouldn't have to worry about anything. I would be at Daunte's house when he played for the Minnesota Vikings, and I would whoop his teammates in a pool game when they stopped by. I didn't care who had the most money or whose name rang the loudest, they could never beat me.

I remember when I beat Randy Moss's agent, whose name was also Daunte, in a game one day. He was an Italian dude who wore the most expensive suits I had ever seen. He was all talk about how he was sure he could whoop me, but I wasn't fazed. By the end of the game, I had that Italian boy sweating through that expensive suit and mad that he was out some money.

Pep (What I call Daunte) and I still laugh about that. He can't believe that I beat the man like that, and I can't believe that he can't believe it. No one knows mercy when it comes to pool and me in the same sentence.

I continued to live life like I was doing. From the outside, it seemed like I was doing everything good, but a toll was being taken on some of my relationships. None more than the relationship with my wife, Sabrina. She had been with me for over a decade. She held me down while I was in prison and helped nurse me back to health when I was shot, but life was getting in the way of us being happy. We started butting heads about all types of things: the kids, my work, and life. So, it was no surprise that she filed for divorce in May 2005.

After Sabrina filed for divorce, it was like my life was going downhill again. I didn't go back to using drugs, but it just seemed like everything started working against me. My legit businesses began to suffer, which meant I had to depend more on the dope game to survive, and that wasn't a good idea at all.

I ended up getting busted for trafficking and manufacturing cocaine in late 2005. I had never been in federal trouble before; all my charges were state, but the United States Government was after me this time. I didn't want to go to federal prison, so I decided that I was going to go on the run. My divorce was finalized in May 2006, and the court date was set for June 10, 2006. I wouldn't be there, though. I would be anywhere else but there.

I knew the feds were watching me to see if I might run, so I knew I couldn't take my car to escape. I also had a friend who worked in trucking. He told me he wanted someone to ride with him while he went to Fort Lauderdale. I knew this would be my chance to escape. My friend didn't think I was on the run, but I had my getaway. I arrived in Fort Lauderdale to stay free as long as I could.

The hardest part about going on the run was not being able to see my kids. I couldn't tell them or their mothers' where I was because, for all I knew, the feds might be listening in on phone calls, and they would know where to find me. I stayed low key in Fort Lauderdale for eight months. I didn't go out much and stayed away from places I was known to be. It was the most time I had spent in my parent's house since childhood. I don't think they thought to look for me there because of that reason.

Over the last month, I had started to miss my kids. I am missing a large part of their lives and can't take it anymore. I told one of my nephews that I would go back to Ocala to see them and then come back and start my life again. So, he agreed to take me back to Ocala that weekend after a basketball game on Friday.

I stood in my mother's front yard that Friday, almost dark outside. It was dark enough for people to have their headlights on while driving, but I noticed two trucks sitting at the end of the street with no lights on. I immediately knew this was the police, and they had found me. I didn't allow them to put on the lights before I started running. I was jumping over gates and running through backyards, but unlike other times, they were prepared for me to run. I had gotten older, and my legs couldn't carry me away fast enough.

The police brought me back to my mother's house, and she was upset. The police had placed my sister, who lived across from my mother, in handcuffs in the back of a squad car, and my mother was about to lose her mind. She didn't even know that I was on the run. I told her I needed to get away and get my life together.

The police ran all my information in the squad car, and my results returned.

"No wonder you were running," the officer said. "You're wanted in Marion County for some things too. What's this about a grand theft charge?"

I sighed, "You got me now. Please let my sister go. My mother doesn't need to see all this. She's old, and it's not good for her."

"But it was good for your mother that you were manufacturing and selling drugs?" he said.

"Just let my sister go," I responded.

I was taken to the county jail, where I was booked on federal charges. I knew that it was better to be picked up on federal charges than on state charges because if you get picked up on federal charges first, the state will run your charges from them concurrently. That way, I could get out at once and not have to serve time consecutively.

I arrived in North Carolina to serve my stint in federal prison in January 2008 to serve a twelve-year sentence. It would be the longest time I had ever spent in jail and the furthest away I would serve from my family. There are over a thousand miles between Florida and North Carolina, but my mother made it along with my kids.

As the months in prison started to go, I finally saw that the life I was living would always end up in the same place. I had already missed parts of my children's lives while they grew up, and I would now miss even more. Living the way I was living wasn't stable, and it wasn't working. Either I would spend the rest of my life in and out of prison, or I would end up dead. I decided I needed to make a change.

I had read the Bible before, but I don't think I understood it correctly. I grew up in church and went with my parents every Sunday, but I never let the message sink in. I was too busy trying to do everything else but be reasonable. The call of the streets was louder than any verse I had heard growing up, but now it was quiet. The voice from the streets was still there, but I didn't want to listen anymore. There was another voice that I could hear now. It was quiet, and it was still. It didn't promise me a flashy lifestyle, but it did promise me peace.

So, I started going to Bible study in jail and turned my life around. The next time my mother visited me, I was so happy to tell her that I had turned my life over to Christ and I was saved. I had never seen my mother cry the way she did that day. She gave all the glory to God and praised him in the visiting room at the prison. I promised her that I would never be back in this place again, and I would show her that I could be an upstanding man when I got out this time.

God had other plans, though. Around 2015, my mother was in and out of the hospital. There was something wrong with her digestive system. I didn't get the full details, but I knew she wasn't doing well. On March 11, 2016, my mother succumbed to her illness. I was so hurt that I wouldn't be there to see her one more time before they put her in her casket.

I wanted to show her I could be the good man she raised me to be, but that wasn't possible anymore. I was mad at everyone, but especially myself. The choices I had made robbed me of spending time with my mother.

Some of my friends taped the funeral and sent it to me. It was a service fit for an angel. They sent my mother home the right way, and it was befitting her all the way through. I was still upset that I couldn't be there, but I was happy that whatever pain she felt was now gone.

So, when I got out in 2018, I vowed to prove what I promised to her. I would be the good man she wanted me to be.

# Chapter 12

I spent ten years and eleven months under the federal government's watch. I did my last six months in a halfway house and was released in January of 2018. I was determined not to let my mother down. So, I went legit. I got an actual job that wouldn't have the police or people wanting to kick my door down. I found a church home to keep me rooted in God's word, so even if I was tempted, I had the tools to fight against the temptations that are out there. And I embraced my new role as a grandparent. I wouldn't miss years of my grandchildren's lives like I did with my children. I would be an example for them.

My children have always loved me. Even when I was away for decisions that I made, I never doubted whether their love changed. I was still their dad, and they would always be mine.

I started working for a company called Profi Maintenance. It was work that I was used to doing during my probation. If you need it done, we do it. From handyman work, pressure washing, street sweeping, and cleanup, ProFi has you covered. It may not bring in the money I'm used to, but it's honest. I don't have to worry about cleaning any of this money through a legitimate business. When I get home, and I'm tired at the end of the day, it's because I've been working and not because I've been running.

Over the years, Stephanie was a constant thought in my mind. I always wondered about what the young woman I was so in love with in 1978 had grown to become. Over the years, I would run into her sporadically. After I moved to Ocala in 1980, we lost touch for the most part. I ran into her at a gas station while visiting Fort Lauderdale in 1989. My wife was pregnant and had just had her first and only child. I didn't see her again until my brother Curtis took me to see her in 2007 because she lived in the same apartment complex as our friend. But I went to prison after that. I thought that would be the end of our story. We had each other once but wouldn't have each other again.

In December 2018, a friend of mine went to a funeral in Fort Lauderdale. While he was there, he called me, "Man, guess who's here?"

"Who?" I said. "Stephanie!" he replied.

It had been almost twelve years since the last time I had spoken to her, and that was only a little while in the car. I knew I couldn't miss this opportunity again.

My friend gave her the phone, and I was instantly transported back to the late 1970s. We talked for a long while and caught up on some things. When my friend got the phone back, he made sure to get Stephanie's number so I could have it.

So, I called her, and we started talking again. Eventually, I started making my way back down to Fort Lauderdale to see her. After 40 years, she still held me in her heart. I wanted to learn everything we had missed about each other over the years. I came to find out that after I left her all those years ago, Stephanie went into a dark depression. I was her first love, and I left her high and dry. My addiction had caused her pain when I was trying to keep it from her. She went through life and had a series of failed relationships, but she still kept a candle burning for me through it all.

After all the things I had done, I didn't think I deserved to be treated or loved like this, but God saw differently. His blessings rain on the just as well as the unjust. I was happy, safe, and in love. So, on April 16, 2022, I made Stephanie my wife. It was one of the best days of my life.

As a married, working, and upstanding citizen, I feel good about myself and life. I love my family and the new path that I'm on. I'm still the baddest man in pool to come out of Florida, and I don't hesitate to remind people where my nickname comes from. For the first time, I feel like I'm finally living the kind of life I'm supposed to live.

I'm getting back into trucking too. I'm opening myself a shop where I'm going to repair trucks and sell truck parts. I can't believe that I am going to China to set up a deal with a tire manufacturer. The best part of this is that it's not funded or held up by drug money in the background. This is all me working with the business mind that I have to make something that my kids and grandkids can be proud of.

I can't lie; I still hear the streets calling me occasionally. But I'm older now, so I also can't listen to them. But sometimes, they get louder when things get a little too hard. My old self starts thinking about how I can turn things around quickly, but I resist the thought. I made a promise to my mother, to my God, and to my wife that I would never go back to a life that would lead me away from my family ever again.

# Acknowledgement

I would like a special acknowledgement to 'Master P" who inspired me to take action in starting my tire business. I would like to also acknowledge my nephew Kelvin Pickney who actually encouraged me to write this book about my life. A special shout out to my Ghost Writer Omega Hagins and of course my good friend and protege "Dante Culpepper" who inspired me through his desire and work ethic to become a professional football player. Lastly I would like to acknowledge Dr. Darrell Tolbert and his V-1 publishing company for making my dream to write a book become a reality!

www.ingramcontent.com/pod-product-compliance
Lightning Source LLC
Chambersburg PA
CBHW052119030426
42335CB00025B/3049